THE
PRESCRIPTION
COMPANION WORKBOOK

Ken Ashley, CCIM, MCR, SIOR

COPYRIGHT

The Prescription Companion Workbook

ISBN eBook: 979-8-89576-193-9
ISBN Print: 979-8-89576-194-6

Published by:
Ashley Publishing LLC (2026)

"It is not the critic who counts; not the man who points out how the strong man stumbles, or where the doer of deeds could have done them better. The credit belongs to the man who is actually in the arena, whose face is marred by dust and sweat and blood; who strives valiantly; who errs, who comes short again and again, because there is no effort without error and shortcoming; but who does actually strive to do the deeds; who knows great enthusiasms, the great devotions; who spends himself in a worthy cause; who at the best knows in the end the triumph of high achievement, and who at the worst, if he fails, at least fails while daring greatly, so that his place shall never be with those cold and timid souls who neither know victory nor defeat."

THEODORE ROOSEVELT

FOREWORD

Breaking into commercial real estate brokerage isn't easy, and succeeding once you're in can be even harder. The path is competitive, the learning curve is steep, and the stakes are high. That's where *The Prescription Companion Workbook* comes in. Designed as the practical companion to *The Prescription*, this hands-on workbook transforms insight into action. It gives aspiring and early-career brokers the structure, exercises, and planning tools needed to turn curiosity about commercial real estate into a real career plan.

Inside, you'll work through the three pillars that shape a successful brokerage career:
Understanding the Industry: Clarify how commercial real estate brokerage really works, the different types of brokers, and where you might fit within the profession.
Getting Hired: Build a concrete strategy to move from interest to opportunity, with guided exercises that help you prepare for interviews, identify the right brokerage culture, and position yourself as a strong candidate.
Succeeding as a Broker: Develop the habits, mindset, and professional roadmap required to thrive in a commission-driven business.

Throughout the workbook, you'll reflect, plan, and document your personal strategy to create your own Prescription. Whether you are still exploring the industry, actively seeking your first brokerage role, or beginning your career, the exercises inside will help you think like a professional broker from day one.

Written from the perspective of a veteran tenant representative who has spent three decades helping companies solve complex real estate problems, this workbook provides the kind of practical guidance rarely shared outside the brokerage floor.

Commercial brokerage rewards initiative, curiosity, and preparation. This workbook helps you bring all three to the table and start building your future in the business.

TABLE OF CONTENTS

HOW TO USE THIS WORKBOOK

This workbook is designed to help you apply the ideas in the book—not just read them. Commercial real estate is a contact sport, and progress happens when you take action, reflect intentionally, and build habits that compound over time. Each exercise in this workbook is structured to help you do exactly that.

1 Complete the exercises in order (if possible).

The book is written as a progression—from understanding the industry, to building your skills, to growing your business. The exercises mirror that progression. You'll get the most benefit if you work through them in sequence.

2 Don't rush. Do the thinking.

Some exercises will take five minutes. Others may take an hour. Give yourself permission to slow down and think deeply. Clarity is a competitive advantage.

3 Be honest with yourself.

This workbook is for you, not your manager, not your mentor, not your colleagues. The only way it works is if you tell the truth in your answers about your goals, skills, gaps, motivations, and habits.

4 Apply immediately.

Every exercise is designed to produce actions you can start taking right now. If you finish an exercise and don't know your next step, go back and refine your answers until your next action is obvious.

5 **Revisit regularly.**

Your career will evolve. Markets will shift. Your perspective will deepen. Return to these exercises every six to twelve months to recalibrate and update your plan.

6 **Use this workbook as a tool, not a textbook.**

You don't need perfect handwriting, pretty notes, or perfectly crafted answers. You need momentum. Think of this as your CRE "training gym"—a place to build skill, discipline, and opportunity.

7 **Make it yours.**

Highlight. Scribble in the margins. Add additional pages. Treat this workbook as a living document that grows with your career.

Most important: 

Your success won't come from reading this book. It will come from doing the work consistently, with clarity and purpose. This workbook is here to help you do exactly that.

> "The secret of change is to focus all of your energy not on fighting the old but on building the new."
> **– Socrates**

FOUNDATIONS OF SUCCESS IN COMMERCIAL REAL ESTATE

YOUR PERSONAL "WHY" STATEMENT

Write a short personal "Why Statement" for your CRE journey. Include motivation, strengths, and desired impact. Consider the following questions when writing your statement.

- **Why do you want to enter CRE now?**

- **What unique strengths do you bring?**

- **What unique experience do you have?**

SELF-ASSESSMENT OF KEY SUCCESS TRAITS

I believe there are core traits required to excel in CRE brokerage, including sales ability, listening, resilience, branding, negotiation, and more. Success requires both personality-driven skills (trust-building, storytelling) and discipline-driven habits (focus, persistence, long-term thinking). To succeed in CRE, you must understand not just the business but yourself. Through decades of personal experience and observation, here are the success attributes that I feel consistently show up among top producers:

Sales Ability	Winning trust and influencing decisions
Marketing	Developing a memorable market brand
Tactical Listening	Listening to understand, not to reply
Focus	Solving client problems, not pushing services
Persistence & Resilience	Staying front-of-mind and bouncing back
Storytelling & Communication	Clarity, charm, and short-form narratives
Networking Skills	Building influence without relying on alcohol
Tech Savvy	Leveraging tools to replace low-value tasks
Negotiation Skills	Constant, lifelong improvement
Market Knowledge	Curiosity-driven mastery of your niche
Long-Term Focus	CRE is a "get-rich-slow" profession
Hustle	The internal drive that no one can teach
Managing Fear	Navigating anxiety until competence appears
Humility	Staying grounded once you succeed

- **Which 3-5 skills are you confident that you already possess?**

- **Which 3 skills do you think you most need to develop?**

- **Name one thing you can do this week to begin working on the development of one of the skills you identified.**

SALES ABILITY & TACTICAL LISTENING

Sales in CRE is less about "pitching" and more about listening, understanding business problems, and communicating value. Tactical listening, the ability to hear what someone means, not just what they say, is a differentiator.

- **Recall a recent conversation where you listened more than you spoke. What did you learn that you would have missed if you dominated the discussion?**

- **How do you currently demonstrate credibility when meeting someone for the first time?**

- **What are three questions you could ask a prospect that demonstrate genuine curiosity about their business rather than your services?**

PERSISTENCE, RESILIENCE & MANAGING FEAR

CRE involves rejection, unpredictable income, emotional pressure, and high stakes. Successful brokers develop routines to manage fear, bounce back quickly, and stay committed even when progress is slow.

- **Think of a time you failed or were rejected. How long did it take you to process that experience, and what helped you move forward?**

- **Which part of CRE do you think will trigger the most anxiety for you: outreach, unpredictable income, or high-pressure negotiations? Why?**

- **List three strategies you could use to manage fear in this business.**

- **Identify one person who could be your "lifeline." How could they help support you in tough moments?**

STORYTELLING, COMMUNICATION & NETWORKING

The best brokers tell short, compelling stories and know how to connect with strangers authentically (not through alcohol or forced schmoozing). Communication is central to winning trust.

- **Write a short "professional story" about who you are and why you're entering CRE. Now, edit that story to 50% of its original length. Practice being succinct while highlighting the most important parts.**

- **What is one story from your life or career that demonstrates your reliability, resilience, or problem-solving ability?**

"Start where you are. Use what you have. Do what you can." – **Arthur Ashe**

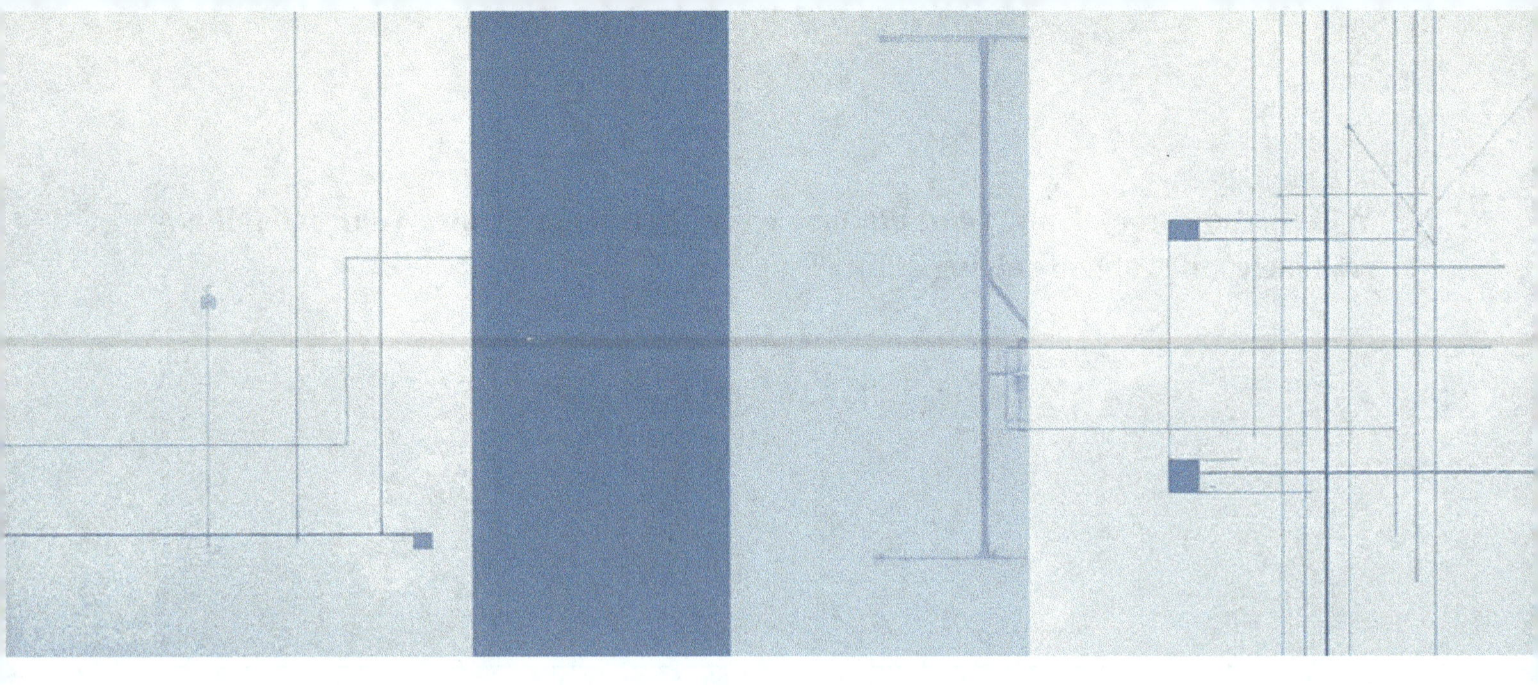

SECTION ONE:
ON UNDERSTANDING COMMERCIAL REAL ESTATE

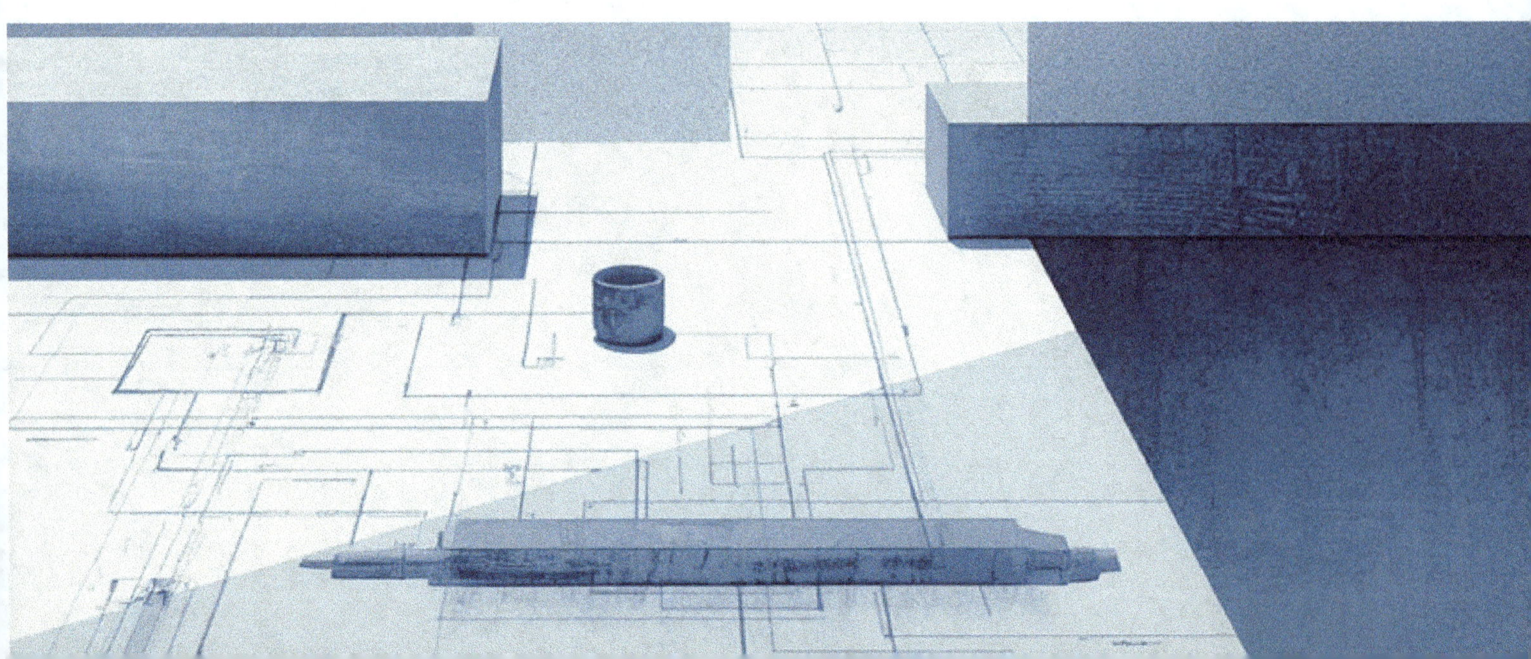

CHAPTER 1: INTRODUCTION TO COMMERCIAL REAL ESTATE

RESIDENTIAL VS. COMMERCIAL: UNDERSTANDING THE MINDSET SHIFT

Residential and commercial real estate operate on very different logic:

- **Residential** = emotional, lifestyle-driven, cash flow is not usually the main goal
- **Commercial** = business proposition, cash flow, investment returns

CRE is fundamentally a business-driven, cash-flow-oriented field. Residential real estate deals are emotional and lifestyle-based, while CRE decisions focus on operational needs, investment returns, and strategic business planning. Chapter 1 outlines major asset types—office, industrial, retail, medical, and data centers—and explains how new brokers gain expertise through mentorship and hands-on learning. Ultimately, the chapter positions CRE as a broad, opportunity-rich profession where value is created by solving business problems, building expertise, and navigating a long-term, high-reward career path.

Read the *Residential vs. Commercial: An Imperfect Comparison* section of Chapter 1, then complete the activities below.

● **Fill in the Venn diagram.**

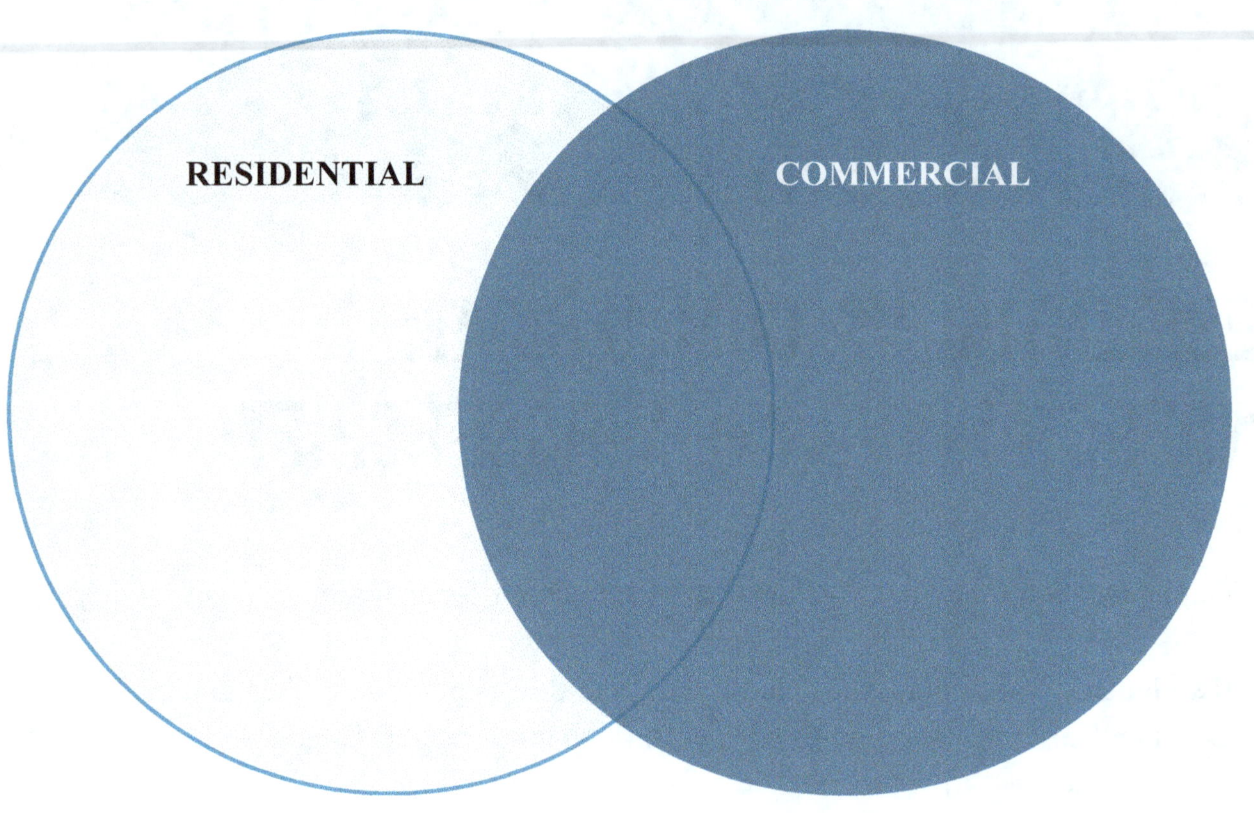

● **Write 3–4 sentences on why commercial real estate's business-first nature appeals to you as a potential broker.**

UNDERSTANDING THE T-BAR: OWNERS VS. CORPORATE USERS

To simplify the industry, the T-Bar model divides the field into Owners (investors, asset managers, property managers, landlord brokers) and Corporate Users (board leadership, executives, real estate directors, tenant representatives), each with unique motivations and decision structures.

THE COMMERCIAL REAL ESTATE T-BAR

OWNERSHIP	CORPORATION
Building ownership/ Ultimate owner	Corporate Tenant
↓	↓
Asset Manager	Board of Directors
↓	↓
Property Manager	Top Executive Resp. for Commercial Real Estate (i.e., CFO)
↓	↓
Leasing Broker	Real Estate Director
	Tenant Representative / Project Manager

- **On the ownership side, describe the responsibilities of:**

Asset manager

Property manager

Landlord broker

- **On the corporate user side, describe the responsibilities of:**

CFO/CAO/COO

Real estate director

Tenant representative

- **Describe how the concept of a "professional real estate investor" differs from a company that simply uses real estate.**

EXPLORING THE "FLAVORS OF ICE CREAM:" CRE ASSET TYPES

Commercial real estate includes asset classes like office, industrial, retail, medical office, and data centers, each with its own learning curve and culture. Review the *Different Types of Commercial Real Estate* section.

- **Which asset type seems most interesting to you right now? Why?**

> You only have to do a few things right in your life so long as you don't do too many things wrong.
> – **Warren Buffett**

- Which asset type seems most intimidating? What skills do you think it would require?

- The chapter mentions the "blacksmith method." Explain what it means and why it matters for new brokers.

- If you had to pick one asset class to apprentice in for your first year, which would you choose? Why?

- **How could you use conferences, senior brokers, and market research to build expertise in a chosen niche?**

HOW CRE BROKERS CREATE VALUE

CRE brokers help companies advance their business, not just find space. Using the entire chapter as your guide, complete the following:

- **Give three examples of how a broker helps a business improve its operations through real estate decisions.**

- **In your own words, describe why CRE is a "get-rich-slow profession."**

- **Explain how your background, interests, or strengths could help you bring value to clients as you grow.**

CHAPTER 2: THE COMMERCIAL REAL ESTATE INDUSTRY

This chapter introduces the scope and structure of commercial real estate (CRE) and how deeply it is embedded in everyday life, from where we work and shop to how goods are stored, distributed, and delivered. The goal of this section is familiarity, not memorization. You are building conceptual awareness of how the industry fits together.

Chapter 2 breaks down major property types (office, retail, industrial, and hospitality), explains how buildings are classified (Class A, B, and C), and introduces the investment side of CRE, including cash flow, appreciation, and tax considerations. It also reinforces that careers in CRE are flexible and evolve over time based on interests, strengths, and risk tolerance.

A DAY IN THE LIFE

Take a typical day in your life, from waking up to going to sleep, and map out every interaction you have with commercial real estate.

- **List each stop or activity (e.g., gym, office, coffee shop, gas station, online shopping delivery).**
- **Next to each, identify what CRE category it belongs to (office, retail, industrial, hospitality, special-purpose).**

Goal: Build awareness of how deeply commercial real estate is woven into everyday routines. Writing full sentences is optional; bullet points or mental walkthroughs are fine.

ACTIVITY	CRE CATEGORY

PROPERTY CLASSIFICATION

This exercise helps you practice applying the Class A/B/C framework to real-world examples. You are not expected to be perfectly accurate—the goal is to think like a market participant.

Choose three buildings in your city, preferably ones you pass regularly.

For each building:
- **Assign it a class (A, B, or C) based on age, condition, and location.**
- **Write 1–2 sentences explaining your reasoning.**

BUILDING	CLASS	EXPLAIN YOUR REASONING

COMMERCIAL REAL ESTATE VOCABULARY MATCH

Match the term in **Column A** with its correct definition or example in **Column B.**

TERM	DEFINITION/EXAMPLE
1. Class A	A. Primarily driven by a business proposition and cash flow.
2. Class B	B. Asset class that is old, outdated, and may be on the edge of building code compliance.
3. Class C	C. Properties that store goods, often featuring high ceiling heights.
4. Industrial	D. An asset class considered "goldilocks" – aging but offering real bargains.
5. Commercial Real Estate (CRE)	E. The top-quality asset class, newer construction, and located at Main and Main.
6. Tax Benefits	G. The government's incentive for investors to create more commercial space.

Chapter 3 offers a detailed look into the daily life and responsibilities of commercial real estate brokers—primarily tenant representatives, but also landlord brokers and capital markets professionals. It explains that a broker's core mission revolves around relationships, market knowledge, and closing deals.

The chapter emphasizes traits necessary for success, such as hustle, resilience, self-confidence, and the ability to handle rejection. It also walks through the typical steps of a tenant-rep assignment, from understanding a client's business challenge to creating a property survey, touring, negotiating, analyzing RFPs, finalizing terms, and supporting the lease process.

Chapter 3 closes by outlining various brokerage career models, contrasting tenant reps with landlord brokers and capital markets brokers, highlighting their responsibilities, skills, and compensation structures.

A DAY IN THE LIFE OF A TENANT REP

Map the Tenant Rep Process

Scenario: A regional law firm needs to relocate its headquarters and asks you to assist as their tenant representative. Complete the following tasks:

1 **List the eight major steps a tenant rep follows (from mandate → tours → RFP → lease review).**

2 **For each step, write one sentence describing what you would be doing for this firm.**

Which step do you believe would be the most challenging for you, and explain why.

BROKERAGE MODELS: UNDERSTANDING YOUR OPTIONS

Commercial real estate brokers typically operate within one of three broad models. This section is about understanding the landscape, not choosing a career path or assessing your skills.

- **Local Market Expert:** Deep expertise in a specific geographic area or submarket.
- **Product Specialist:** Specialized knowledge in a particular asset type (for example: medical office, data centers, industrial).
- **Account Specialist:** Serving the full real estate needs of a single client or corporate account.

Which model seems most interesting to you right now, and why? This is not a commitment, as career specialization evolves over time.

PERSONAL RISK TOLERANCE TOOL

Your ability to thrive in different commercial real estate roles often depends on how much uncertainty, variability, and financial pressure you're comfortable handling. This short questionnaire will help you understand your personal risk tolerance so you can better identify which CRE paths may be the best fit for you. Commercial real estate, especially brokerage, often requires delayed gratification, emotional resilience, and comfort with income variability. It is normal for early-career professionals to supplement income with savings or a second job.

Rate each item from 1 (Strongly Disagree) to 5 (Strongly Agree).

1. I am comfortable with a career in which income can be inconsistent.
2. I can stay motivated even when results take months or years to materialize.
3. I am willing to take calculated risks to achieve long-term rewards.
4. I can manage stress when facing financial uncertainty.
5. I adapt quickly to changing market conditions.
6. I have a financial buffer or plan to handle low-income periods.
7. I enjoy entrepreneurial work where results depend on my own efforts.
8. I can maintain confidence after hearing "no" repeatedly.
9. I am willing to invest time into relationships that may not pay off immediately.
10. I feel confident making decisions without having all available information.

Scoring Guide:

- **40–50:** High risk tolerance: well-suited for brokerage.
- **25–39:** Moderate risk tolerance: can succeed with structure, mentorship, and planning.
- **10–24:** Low risk tolerance: consider hybrid or salaried CRE roles.

Chapter 4 explains how commercial real estate brokers earn money and why brokerage can be one of the highest-income career paths in the industry. It outlines compensation structures across tenant representation, landlord representation, and capital markets brokerage, including how fees are generated, who pays them, and how brokerage splits affect take-home earnings. The chapter also compares large, mid-sized, and local brokerage firms and how each model influences training, resources, culture, and long-term earning potential.

For detailed explanations of compensation structures, fee theory, and brokerage economics, refer back to Chapter 4 in the book. The exercises below are designed to help you apply those concepts.

STEP-BY-STEP COMPENSATION MATH (APPLIED CALCULATION)

Use the compensation principles explained in Chapter 4 to calculate earnings in a realistic deal. To keep things simple, let's look at a transaction with one broker and a simple 50/50 split with the brokerage house. For a 10,000-square-foot office lease at $45 per square foot per year with a 3% escalation each year over 5 years, the fee earned at 4% is just under $100,000. After your split with the brokerage house, you pocket just under $50,000 from a single transaction.

Office Lease Transaction: 5-Year Rent and Broker Earnings

Annual Rent with 3% Escalation (10,000 sq ft at $45/sq ft)

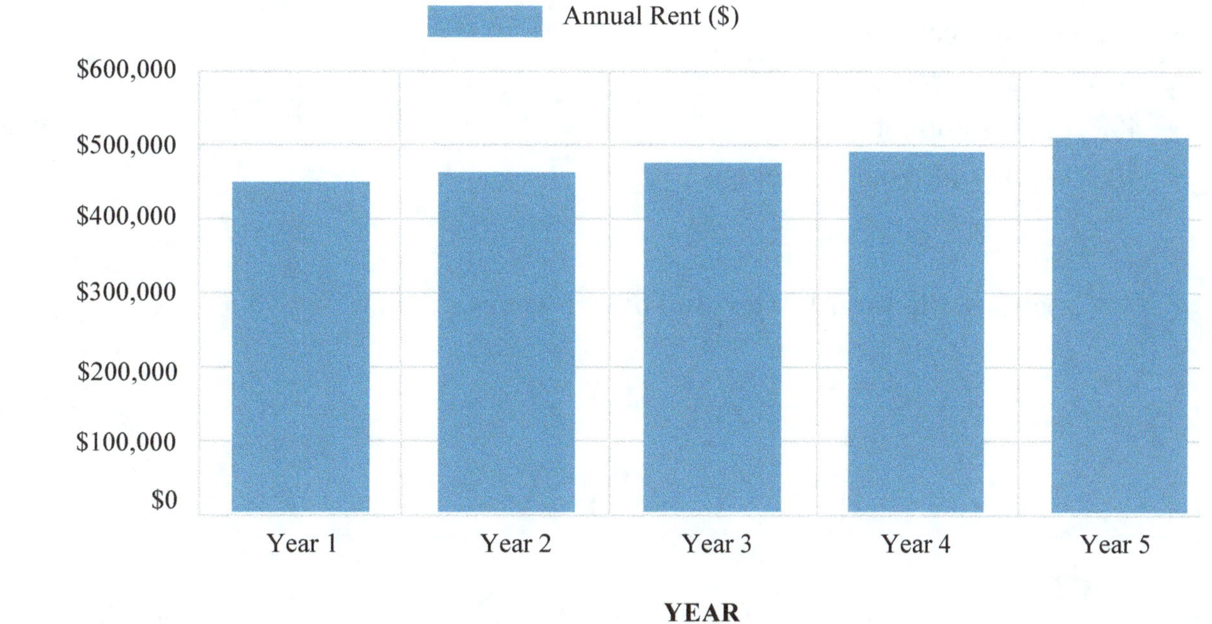

Metric	Amount ($)
Total Rent (5 Years)	2,389,111.11
Broker Fee (4%)	98,564.44
Broker's Share (50%)	47,782.22

You are a tenant representative helping a client sign:

- 8,000 square feet
- $40 per square foot per year
- 3% annual escalation
- 5-year lease term
- 4% commission rate
- 50/50 split with your brokerage

1   **Calculate the total lease value over 5 years.**

2   **Multiply total lease value by 4% to determine the gross commission.**

3   **Apply your 50/50 split to determine your take-home pay.**

REFLECTION

- **How does this exercise change your perspective on CRE earning potential?**

- **What excites you most about commission-based compensation?**

- **What concerns you most about commission-based compensation?**

- **Based on your temperament, does commission-only compensation feel motivating or stressful?**

- **Which broker type feels most aligned with your comfort level right now?**
  - **Tenant Rep**
  - **Landlord Rep**
  - **Capital Markets Broker**

BROKERAGE SHOP COMPARISON MATRIX

Use this matrix to compare brokerage platforms using information from the chapter.

Focus on evaluating:
- Training quality
- Mentorship access
- Market data and tools
- Brand strength
- Culture and collaboration
- Long-term career support

Note: Commission split is only one factor, and often not the most important one, early in a career.

	Large Global Firm (e.g., Cushman & Wakefield, CBRE, JLL)	Mid-Sized Firm (Regional or National)	Local Boutique Shop
Commission Split Tendencies			
Types of Resources/Support Offered			
Brand Power and Perceived Credibility			
Level of Independence Required			
Pros and Cons for Someone Early in Their CRE Career	Pros: Cons:	Pros: Cons:	Pros: Cons:

CHAPTER 5: OCCUPIER: REASONS COMPANIES LEASE SPACE

This chapter explains why companies lease space and why understanding those reasons is essential for commercial real estate brokers. While buying real estate can make sense in specific situations—such as for specialized facilities, long-term occupancy, or small owner-operated firms—most companies lease because it preserves capital, offers flexibility, and reduces operational burdens. The chapter outlines key leasing considerations, including location, layout, costs, lease terms, amenities, and building management. It also explores why office space remains relevant post-COVID, emphasizing four core drivers: culture, accountability, learning, and the speed of business. Ultimately, brokers must understand both the business imperatives behind real estate decisions and how to align space solutions with a company's strategic goals.

CONCEPT CHECK: MULTIPLE CHOICE & SHORT ANSWER

Select the BEST answer for each question.

1. Companies most commonly lease space instead of buying because:
a. Leasing is more fun
b. Leasing offers greater flexibility and moderates upfront costs
c. Leasing is legally required for office users
d. Buying is only allowed for companies with $10B+ in revenue

2. Which of the following is least likely to buy real estate?
a. A specialized manufacturing company
b. A data center operator
c. A small business owned by one individual
d. A mid-size consulting firm needing flexibility

3. What is considered the "magic number" for buying real estate, according to the chapter?

a. 5 years

b. 10 years

c. 20 years

d. 50 years

4. List two major drawbacks of a company owning its own building.

    1.

    2.

5. What are the four key reasons employers continue to lease office space post-COVID?

    1.

    2.

    3.

    4.

REAL-WORLD SCENARIO: LEASE OR BUY?

You are advising a tech company with 900 employees. They currently occupy two leased floors in a Class A building. The company is growing quickly, adding 150 employees each year. **The CEO asks whether they should buy a building rather than continue leasing. Using the content from the chapter, answer the following:**

- **Should the company buy or lease? (Choose one and defend your answer in 2–3 sentences.)**

- **Identify three factors from the chapter that heavily influence your recommendation.**

- **What risks does rapid growth create for a company that owns its real estate?**

SECTION TWO:
ON GETTING HIRED

Section Two is designed to move you from interest to readiness for real-world execution. It translates the book's ideas into practical behaviors: getting hired, preparing for meetings, building professional relationships, evaluating brokerage offers, and beginning to design a long-term success strategy. The goal is not memorization; it is to help you understand how the commercial real estate industry actually operates day to day and how you personally fit into it.

This section also reinforces momentum-building habits. You will practice planning, outreach, preparation, follow-up discipline, decision-making, and early-stage business development. By the end of the section, you should feel less like a student studying CRE and more like an emerging professional who can plan, communicate value, build relationships, and make informed career decisions.

CHAPTER 6: THE ROAD TO GETTING HIRED IN COMMERCIAL REAL ESTATE BROKERAGE

Chapter 6 breaks down the process of entering the commercial real estate brokerage market into clear, actionable steps, from building a strong business plan to scheduling meetings with brokerages and decision-makers. Success requires preparation, persistence, and the ability to provide value rather than ask for favors. It explains the importance of a simple but effective business development plan, outlines four prospecting approaches (Submarket, Radius, Vertical, Size), and teaches practical outreach skills, including phone scripts, voicemail strategies, digital communication etiquette, and the power of "small promises." Ultimately, the chapter empowers aspiring brokers to get off the couch, build momentum, and secure meetings that lead to opportunities.

THE PRESCRIPTION WORKSHEET

At its core, The Prescription summarizes the "diagnosis" of your professional health, identifying strengths such as strong communication skills or relevant prior experience, while pinpointing areas for improvement, including gaps in market knowledge, networking deficiencies, or the need for practical hustle. Meet with a mentor or trusted friend to make this "diagnosis" of your own situation.

It then prescribes a series of targeted next steps to "cure" these gaps, helping you become smarter about the CRE landscape. This includes educational actions to deepen your understanding of industry trends, such as researching office market dynamics or subscribing to key newsletters; skill-building exercises like practicing negotiation tactics or tactical listening; and strategic moves to position yourself for employment, from updating your LinkedIn profile and attending networking events to applying for internships at brokerage firms.

Presented in a simple, editable worksheet format with columns for Item, Notes, Due Date, and Complete, the Prescription encourages accountability and progress tracking. You can check off completed items, add notes on learnings or challenges, and adjust as needed, turning abstract ambitions into a tangible timeline. Typically spanning 9-15 tasks over a few weeks or months, it's flexible enough to tailor to your pace, whether you're a recent graduate hustling part-time or someone balancing a full-time job.

The ultimate purpose is to foster delayed gratification through consistent execution: by following the Prescription, you'll build a robust network, gain real-world exposure, and demonstrate the initiative that CRE leaders value, ultimately increasing your chances of landing a role at a top firm.

Think of it as your personalized accelerator. Not a magic pill, but a proven regimen to diagnose, educate, and activate your path to becoming a successful tenant rep broker in today's evolving market.

> Far and away the best prize that life offers is the chance to work hard at work worth doing.
> **– Theodore Roosevelt**

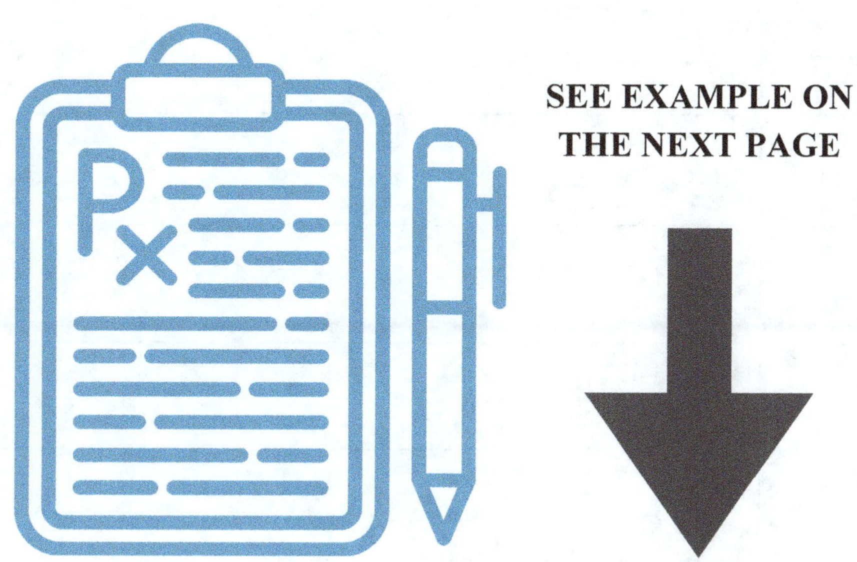

SEE EXAMPLE ON THE NEXT PAGE

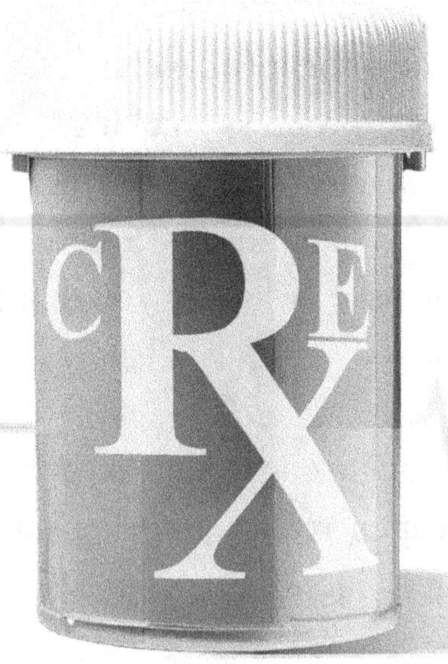

PRESCRIPTION FOR SUCCESS IN
COMMERCIAL REAL ESTATE BROKERAGE

	ITEM	NOTES	DUE DATE	COMPLETE
01	Research and understand the role of a tenant representative in commercial real estate	Read articles or watch videos on tenant rep basics, note down 5 key skills.	June 10	✔
02				
03				
04				
05				
06				
07				
08				
09				
10				
11				

SIGNATURE: _Ken Ashley_

THE PRESCRIPTION WORKSHEET

The chapter emphasizes that securing a job in commercial real estate brokerage is a proactive process. Success comes from having a simple, focused plan and executing it consistently, through research, outreach, phone calls, small promises, and follow-ups. The goal isn't to ask for a job, but to show value, professionalism, and initiative.

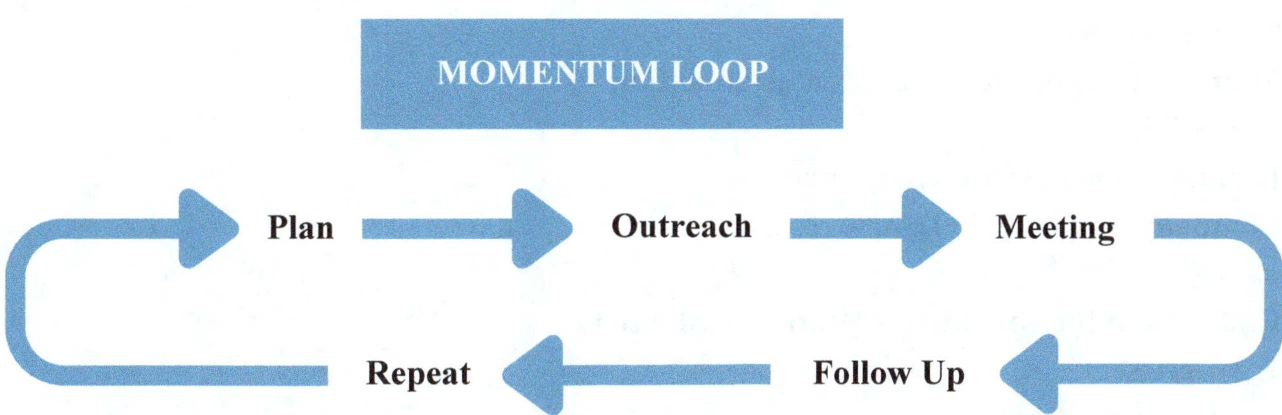

- **Which tactic from this chapter are you most likely to execute in the next 7 days? Why?**

- **Which part of the hiring process do you currently avoid or delay most (planning, outreach, calls, follow-up)? What is one small action you could take this week to reduce that friction?**

BUSINESS PLAN BUILDER

A simple, clear business plan is the foundation for entering the industry. You don't need a thick, complicated plan; just a practical one: identify a focus area, understand your target decision-maker's worries, communicate your value, and lay out the tools you'll use to reach people consistently.

<u>Here is a sample plan from the book:</u>

Area of Focus:______
Type of Commercial Real Estate Brokerage Services: (Office, Industrial, etc.)
Target Executive: (Avatar)
Name: John Smith
Position: CEO of mid-sized manufacturing firm
Age: 45-55
Location: San Francisco Bay Area
Company Size: 100-500 employees

Understand the Executive's Worries and Needs
1. Worries:
- Rising operational costs
- Inefficient use of existing real estate assets
- Market volatility and its impact on property values

2. Needs:
- Cost-effective real estate solutions
- Expert advice on optimizing current properties
- Strategies for future growth and expansion

Capabilities to Solve the Executive's Problems
3. Brokerage Team Strengths:
- Extensive market knowledge and analysis
- Proven track record of cost-saving strategies
- Strong negotiation skills to secure favorable terms
- Comprehensive understanding of property optimization
- Network of industry contacts and resources

Tactics to Reach Out

1. Cold Calls:

○ Aim to make 30 targeted calls per week

○ Use a script focused on understanding the executive's current challenges

2. Social Media LinkedIn Outreach:

○ Connect with executives and share relevant industry insights

○ Post weekly articles and updates on market trends

3. Email Campaigns:

○ Send personalized emails highlighting specific solutions

○ Follow up with case studies and success stories

4. Networking Events:

○ Attend industry conferences and local business events

○ Engage in meaningful conversations and exchange business cards

Goals for Tactics

● **Calls:** 30 calls per week, aiming for a 10% response rate

● **LinkedIn:** 5 new connections per week, 1 post per week

● **Emails:** 20 emails per week, aiming for a 15% open rate

● **Events:** Attend 1 event per month, aiming to secure 5 new contacts per event

Recording Activity

● **Spreadsheet:**

○ Columns: Date, Contact Name, Company, Position, Method of Contact, Response, Follow-Up Date

○ Update daily to ensure accurate tracking of interactions and outcomes

Accountability Function

● **Weekly Reporting:**

○ Submit a report to the senior broker every Friday by 3 PM

○ Include metrics on calls made, emails sent, LinkedIn activity, and events attended

○ Highlight successes and areas for improvement

Campaign Duration
- **Length:** 6 months
- **Review:** Quarterly assessments to evaluate progress and adjust tactics as necessary

Success Metrics
- **Contact Goals:**
  - 50 contacts per week, totaling 1,300 over 6 months
  - Target a 3% success rate to secure 39 meetings

Aim to convert 10% of meetings into transactions, resulting in approximately 4 deals. Use the blank template below to create your own plan.

TEMPLATE

Fill in the template below based on the example above.

Area of Focus:

Type of Commercial Real Estate Brokerage Service:

Target Executive:

Name:

Position:

Age:

Location:

Company Size:

Executive's Worries:

Executive's Needs:

Brokerage Team Strengths:

Cold Call Script: (Aim for 30 targeted calls per week - 10% response rate)

Social Media LinkedIn Outreach Script:

Email Campaign Script: (20 emails per week - aiming for 15% open rate)

List of Networking Events to Attend: (1 event per month)

CRAFT THE PERFECT PHONE SCRIPT

Get out there and meet people. Treat your first three to five conversations as advice meetings. Talk to executives, learn how they got started, and get guidance on launching your career. After that, shift into "hunting" mode: keep asking questions, but focus on building relationships that can lead to a job.

Use business journals, industry sites, and LinkedIn to find leaders. If you share a connection, ask for an intro. If reaching out cold, don't ask for a job; that's a net-taker move. Instead, focus on what they need and show how you add value. Being a net giver gets you further.

Phone calls still work. Call to ask for advice, share value, and build rapport. Keep it concise and confident, centered on a simple Minimum Viable Question, such as asking for times for a future meeting.

Your Script (3–4 sentences):

OUTREACH STRATEGY: VOICEMAIL & DIGITAL MESSAGING

Effective outreach is about consistency, clarity, and "small promises." The chapter shows how short voicemails, brief LinkedIn messages, and simple follow-ups create momentum and build trust. Keep everything short, respectful, and execution-focused.

Write a Short Voicemail (Under 20 seconds):

Write a 30-Word LinkedIn DM:

List Your Next Three Follow-Up Times:

Follow up 1:

Follow up 2:

Follow up 3:

CHAPTER 7: SETTING THE STAGE: RESEARCH AND PREPARATION FOR THE INTERVIEW

This chapter guides you through the essential steps to preparing for and excelling in a commercial real estate brokerage interview. The process begins with in-depth research on the interviewer, the firm, its producers, and its culture. You then prepare meaningful questions to demonstrate curiosity and business intelligence. During the meeting, you focus on making a strong first impression, active listening, note-taking, personal storytelling, and the 70/30 rule. Finally, you close with a clear next step and follow up professionally. Preparation, presence, and purposeful conversation are the tools that set you apart.

BUILD YOUR PRE-INTERVIEW RESEARCH PLAN

Before the meeting, you must conduct thorough research at both the individual and company levels. This activity helps you organize that research so you walk in informed, confident, and credible.

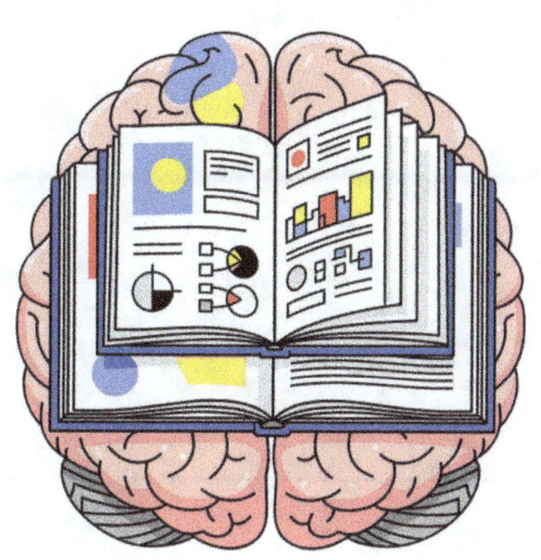

RESEARCH CHECKLIST:

RESEARCHER:	INTERVIEWER:

Your Exercise:

Fill in each section with what you plan to investigate, and then write down your actual findings.

Interviewer Research
- Tenure & specialty
- Awards or accomplishments
- Career path highlights
- Shared connections or interests
- Social media insights

Company Research
- Mission/vision/values
- Main service lines
- Major clients or deals
- Growth plans or recent announcements
- Top producers and what they're known for

WRITE YOUR FIVE POWER QUESTIONS

Your questions signal preparation, maturity, and genuine interest. They should be about them—their leadership, their success, and their goals.

Write five sharp, leadership-oriented questions you will ask during the meeting.

1.

2.

3.

4.

5.

CRAFT YOUR THREE PERSONAL STORIES

Great interviews contain memorable stories: examples of overcoming obstacles, succeeding in sales, performing athletically, or serving your community. This activity helps you prepare your "ready-to-tell" stories.

For each story, write a short version (5–6 sentences) that highlights the challenge, action, and result. Remember, stories should be concise, impactful, and under 3 minutes long.

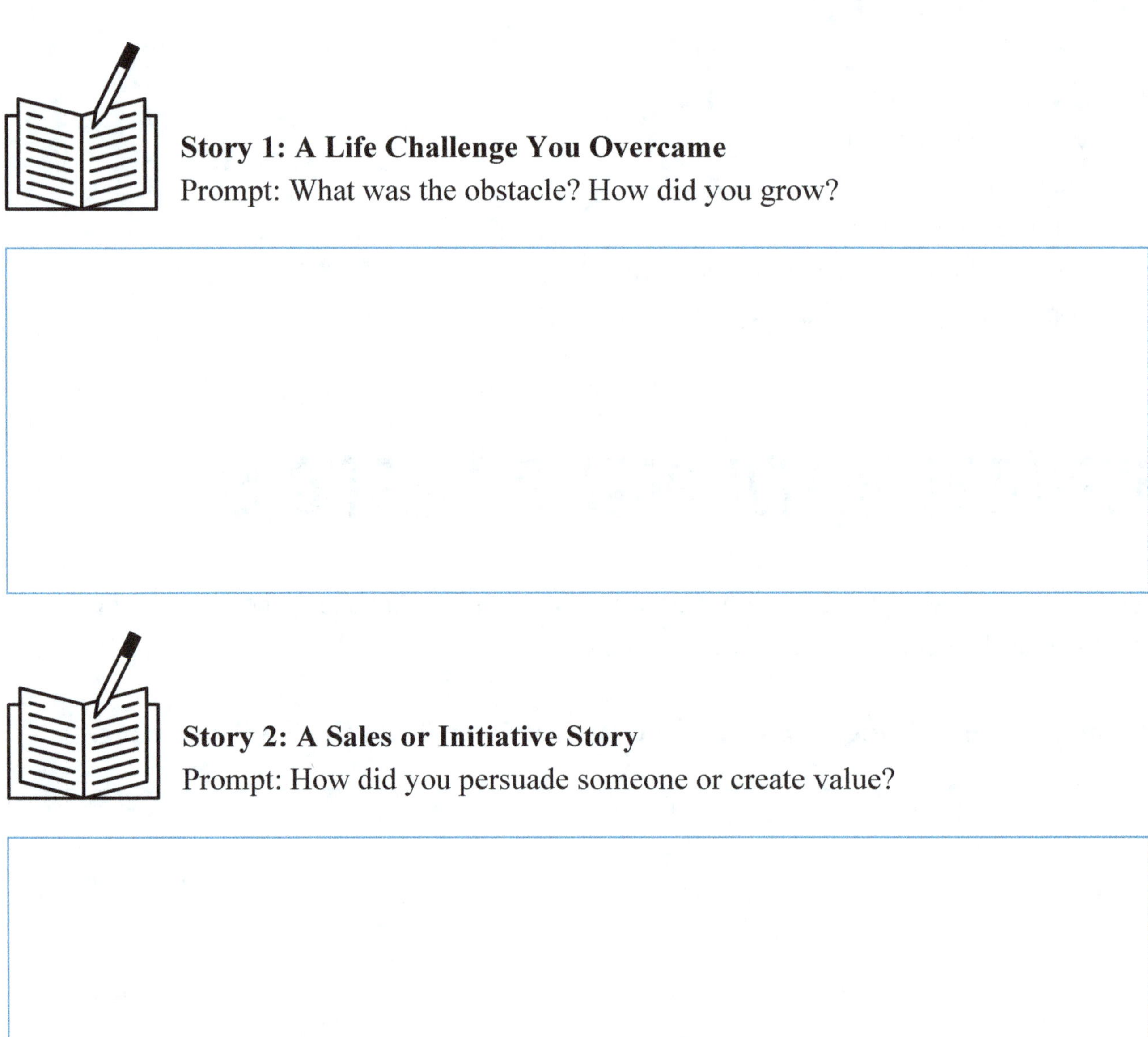

Story 1: A Life Challenge You Overcame
Prompt: What was the obstacle? How did you grow?

Story 2: A Sales or Initiative Story
Prompt: How did you persuade someone or create value?

Story 3: Leadership, Athletics, or Community Story
Prompt: What role did you play? What impact did you have?

FIRST-IMPRESSION ROLE PLAY (BEHAVIORAL PRACTICE)

The first 90 seconds of your meeting carry outsized importance. This exercise helps you practice your opener, handshake, and rapport-building language.

Complete the scripted prompts as if you're rehearsing for the meeting.

A. Your Opening Line When You First Meet the Interviewer:

B. Your First Rapport-Building Statement (LinkedIn, mutual interest, office detail, etc.):

C. Your Note-Taking Statement (if needed):

D. Your Closing Line:

BUILD YOUR INTERVIEW DAY CHECKLIST

A professional, calm, organized interview day happens when you follow a clear checklist. This activity turns the chapter's guidance into a personalized plan.

Your Exercise: Create Your Checklist

Check off items as completed before and during the interview. Add any additional items you feel are relevant to your particular situation.

Pre-Meeting (Day Before):

☐ Confirm time, location, and parking

☐ Review LinkedIn and company research

☐ Print or prepare notebook + pen

☐ Choose and inspect attire

☐ Write a confirmation email

Day Of:

☐ Arrive 30 minutes early

☐ Review notes in the car

☐ Silence phone and store it away

☐ Greet receptionist warmly

☐ Maintain confident posture and eye contact

☐ Take notes visibly and respectfully

☐ Use the 70/30 rule

☐ Ask leadership-focused questions

☐ Close with a next-step commitment

Post-Meeting:

☐ Leave premises before discussing meeting

☐ Voice-dictate notes immediately

☐ Write a thank-you note within 24 hours

CHAPTER 8: LONG TERM LOW PRESSURE FOLLOW UP: MAKE THEM REMEMBER YOU, PRO STYLE

The hardest part of launching your career is getting the first meeting; the second hardest is being remembered afterward. This chapter argues that real relationship power comes from follow-up, not the meeting itself. Strong follow-up starts before you ever talk, by finding a shared "theme" to anchor future touches.

Since executives are flooded with email, handwritten notes stand out. The chapter recommends a simple three-touch system: a same-day thank-you, a personal-interest follow-up tied to your shared theme, and a professional, industry-related touch that shows growing insight. Staying consistent, organized, and respectful builds trust and leads to more meetings.

A Meet Sheet—a basic flat-file CRM—helps track relationships, follow-ups, and lessons learned. With discipline and genuine curiosity, your network becomes a lasting asset.

FINDING YOUR FOLLOW-UP THEME (REFLECTION + RESEARCH)

Follow-up begins before the first meeting. The best follow-up includes a personal theme, something you and the executive share. This shared thread becomes the backbone of your handwritten notes, creating memorability that email alone cannot achieve.

The best investment is in the tools of one's own trade."
– **Benjamin Franklin**

Research your target contact. List 3–5 potential common themes you could use in future follow-ups:

- Shared school or hometown
- Sports
- Childhood organizations
- Hobbies
- Clubs or associations
- Faith or community involvement

Write your list here:

1.

2.

3.

4.

5.

DESIGNING YOUR THREE-TOUCH FOLLOW-UP PLAN (PLANNING WORKSHEET)

The chapter outlines a structured three-step follow-up system: a same-day handwritten thank-you, a thematic article and note 10 days later, and a business-relevant article and note 10 days after that. It builds familiarity and sets up your next meeting request.

Touches	Timing	Purpose	What You Will Send	Notes
Touch 1	Same Day	Gratitude, professionalism, and fast follow-up	Handwritten thank-you note	
Touch 2	+10 Days	Personal connection; memorability	Printed article + handwritten note ("Thought of you…")	
Touch 3	+10 Days	Industry engagement that demonstrates learning	CRE-related article + note referencing business line	

Next Scheduled Outreach Dates:

Touch 1:

Touch 2:

Touch 3:

WRITING YOUR HANDWRITTEN NOTES

Short notes—never emails—cut through the noise, show sincerity, and set you apart. The messaging is simple: personal, brief, no ask.

Draft the three notes that can easily be customized.

1   **Thank-You Note Draft:**

2   **Theme Article Note Draft:**

3   **CRE Article Note Draft:**

PERSISTENCE TRACKING CALENDAR (BEHAVIOR TRACKING)

Consistency and politeness win. Following up every 10 days—brief, positive, and respectful—creates momentum and builds your brand. Most people quit too soon; your consistency is what sets you apart.

Fill out this 10-day contact calendar, then use it to create a full 30-day calendar:

Date	Touch Type	Method	Completed?	Next Step
		Mail/Hand delivery /Email	Yes / No	
		Mail/Hand delivery /Email	Yes / No	
		Mail/Hand delivery /Email	Yes / No	
		Mail/Hand delivery /Email	Yes / No	
		Mail/Hand delivery /Email	Yes / No	
		Mail/Hand delivery /Email	Yes / No	
		Mail/Hand delivery /Email	Yes / No	
		Mail/Hand delivery /Email	Yes / No	
		Mail/Hand delivery /Email	Yes / No	
		Mail/Hand delivery /Email	Yes / No	

BUILD YOUR MEET SHEET (TEMPLATE + REFLECTION)

Your Meet Sheet is a simple but powerful tool—a flat-file CRM where you track whom you've met, when, what you learned, and how you followed up. It demonstrates organization, professionalism, and listening skills.

Name					
Company					
Title					
Date Met					
How We Met					
Key Insights / What I Learned					
Follow-Up Completed?	Yes / No	Yes / No	Yes / No	Yes / No	Yes / No
Next Follow-Up Date					
Notes					

RELATIONSHIP INSIGHTS REFLECTION

Every meeting teaches you something: industry knowledge, character insights, patterns of success. The chapter stresses the value of journaling these lessons to build confidence and accelerate growth.

After each meeting, answer the following:

What did I learn from this person?

What surprised me?

What follow-up theme did I discover?

What's my next step with this relationship?

SCRIPT LIBRARY

This resource is not an exercise, but rather a resource to return to when creating your own scripts. All scripts can be used as-is or modified to match tone and personality.

SCRIPT 1: Thank-You Note

Classic:

"John, thank you again for taking the time to meet with me today. I appreciate the insights you shared and the generous advice. I look forward to continuing to learn from you."

Personalized:

"John, thank you for meeting with me today. I really enjoyed our conversation, especially the story about _________. Your guidance was extremely helpful."

SCRIPT 2: Theme Article Note ("Thought of You…")

Version A:

"John, I came across this article and immediately thought of you. Hope it brings a smile. Wishing you well!"

Version B:

"John, saw this and thought of our conversation. No need to respond, I just wanted to send something I think you'd enjoy."

SCRIPT 3: CRE Article Note

Version A:

"John, I've been paying attention to the _________ business line you mentioned in our meeting. Glad to see the momentum in the sector. I'll reach out soon. I would love to get your advice on my updated business plan."

Version B:

"John, this piece reminded me of our discussion and the trends you're seeing. I've been studying the market and look forward to checking in soon to get your thoughts."

Direct & Respectful:

"John, I hope you've been well. Would you have availability for a quick 30-minute check-in? Here are three times that work on my end:

• Tuesday at 7:45 AM

• Wednesday at 1:00 PM

• Thursday at 9:00 AM

Happy to adjust to whatever works for you."

Light & Polite:

"John, hope your week is off to a good start. I'd love to get your advice on the next version of my plan. If helpful, here are a few times I can be in your office:

• _______

• _______

• _______

Thanks again for your time and mentorship."

1. "Just checking in. I hope you're well."
2. "Still thinking about your advice. Thank you again."
3. "Saw something that reminded me of our conversation—sending it your way soon."
4. "Hope business is strong this month."
5. "Still eager to learn from you. Sending good energy your way."

"The only place where success comes before work is in the dictionary." – **Vidal Sassoon**

CHAPTER 9: I GOT AN OFFER LETTER! WHAT SHOULD I DO NEXT?

Congratulations! You've earned one or more offer letters, and that is a major accomplishment. But now the real decision-making begins. Choosing your first commercial real estate brokerage shapes your development, your income trajectory, and the mentors who will guide you. This chapter outlines eleven critical areas to evaluate before signing: compensation, benefits, culture, research, training, mentorship, support, and more. By scoring each firm on a standardized 1–5 scale and comparing them side by side, you ensure you're making a data-driven decision, not an emotional one. The goal of this section is to help you slow down, think objectively, and choose the environment that gives you the highest probability of long-term success.

COMPENSATION & PERFORMANCE EVALUATION

Compensation is more than just commission splits. It includes draws, salary support, performance expectations, required administrative tasks, expense management, and opportunities to invest in deals. Understanding the full picture allows you to predict early income and avoid unpleasant surprises.

Compensation Evaluation

Rate 1–5 (1 = unhappy, 5 = very happy)

Compensation Factor	Notes	Score (1–5)
Commission split		
Salary/ramp support		
Draw terms (forgivable? interest?)		
Early income opportunities		
Ability to invest in firm deals		
Performance metrics & expectations		

BENEFITS REVIEW

Benefits Evaluation

Benefit Type	Notes	Score (1–5)
Health insurance		
Dental / Vision		
Disability (short & long term)		
Additional benefits (pet insurance, wellness, etc.)		
Cost to you / affordability		

Health insurance, disability coverage, dental, vision, and even pet insurance matter more than most first-year brokers expect. Disability coverage can be especially critical—one accident can derail a year of momentum.

TEAM DYNAMICS & MENTORSHIP COMMITMENT

The people you sit with define your learning curve. Chemistry matters. Mentorship must be explicit, written, and time-bound; otherwise, it will fade. Reverse mentorship opportunities strengthen the relationship.

Team & Mentorship Evaluation

Category	Notes	Score (1–5)
Team chemistry/personality fit		
Trust and communication		
Mentor commitment (formalized?)		
Reverse mentorship opportunities		
Senior leader accessibility		

CULTURE & BRAND

A firm's culture determines whether you grow or burn out. Brand matters because you will attach your name to theirs. Conduct online research, seek external opinions, and carefully evaluate reputation.

Culture & Brand Evaluation

Culture Factor	Notes	Score (1–5)
Office energy & positivity		
Pressure vs. support level		
Mission/vision/values in action		
Marketplace reputation		
Brand strength & alignment with your identity		

TOOLKIT, TECHNOLOGY & OFFICE SPACE

Your toolkit dictates your efficiency. This includes CRM tools, marketing support, databases, AI tools, and the physical workspace. A brokerage that invests in tools accelerates your pipeline.

Tools & Office Evaluation

Technology / Resources	Notes	Score (1–5)
CRM quality		
Marketing tools		
Real estate data systems		
AI availability (protected/private)		
Quality of workspace		
Quiet spaces/flexibility		

RESEARCH SUPPORT

Research teams provide market intelligence, comps, and custom analysis. Strong research allows you to bring insights—not guesses—to clients, especially early on.

Research Evaluation

Technology / Resources	Notes	Score (1–5)
CRM quality		
Marketing tools		
Real estate data systems		
AI availability (protected/private)		
Quality of workspace		
Quiet spaces/flexibility		

TRAINING QUALITY

Never assume a brokerage offers structured training. Preview the material, check the frequency, and see whether they will fund outside training, such as CCIM, SIOR, LinkedIn Learning, or coaching programs.

Training Evaluation

Training Category	Notes	Score (1–5)
Internal training quality		
Availability/frequency		
External training support		
Skill relevance		
Cost (free or subsidized?)		

ADMINISTRATIVE & MARKETING SUPPORT

Administrative and marketing staff can dramatically increase your productivity. Even if you're new, understanding their availability is critical.

Admin & Marketing Evaluation

Support Category	Notes	Score (1–5)
Access to administrative support		
Quality of marketing materials		
Ability to support pitch creation		
Availability/workload of support teams		

FIRMWIDE RESOURCES

A firm with multiple service lines expands your earning potential through referrals and enhances your client offering.

Firm Resources Evaluation

Resource	Notes	Score (1–5)
Number of service lines		
Ability to refer work & earn fees		
Access to experts & specialists		
Additional internal services (PM, workplace, etc.)		

SUPPORT FOR YOUR BUSINESS PLAN

Your business plan must align with the team's vision. Misalignment creates friction and confusion. Ensure leadership explicitly supports and signs off on your plan.

Business Plan Alignment

Alignment Factor	Notes	Score (1–5)
Leadership buy-in		
Team alignment		
Success metrics		
Reporting expectations		

SCHEDULE EXPECTATIONS

Clarify in-office expectations, flexible hours, and work-from-home policies. You will be working long hours, so understand what "normal" is.

Schedule Factor

Alignment Factor	Notes	Score (1–5)
In-office expectations		
Flexibility		
Leader expectations		
Personal alignment		

This is a graphical example of your evaluation of the brokerages you are considering. Taking the time to do a deep dive and your best "look" into the various options will help you (a) make the best choice for you and (b) know that after you start, you made a data-based decision. Your brokerage choice is crucial to your success, and you will operate with immense confidence knowing you've chosen the best option for you in your market.

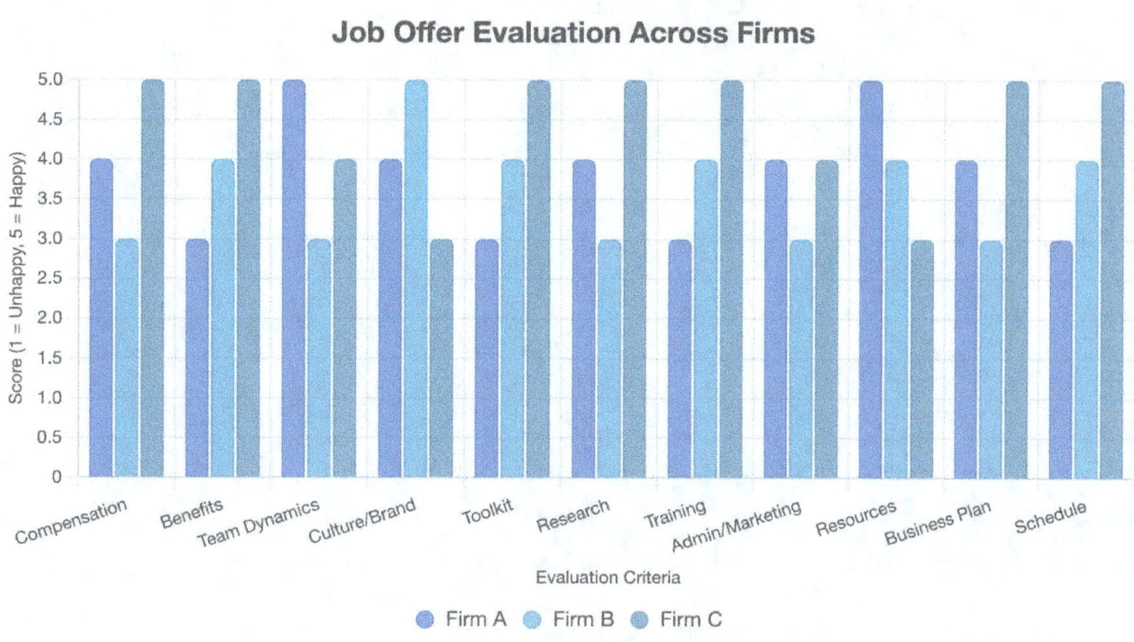

Once you have completed the evaluation above, plot your own answers on the blank version of the bar graph below.

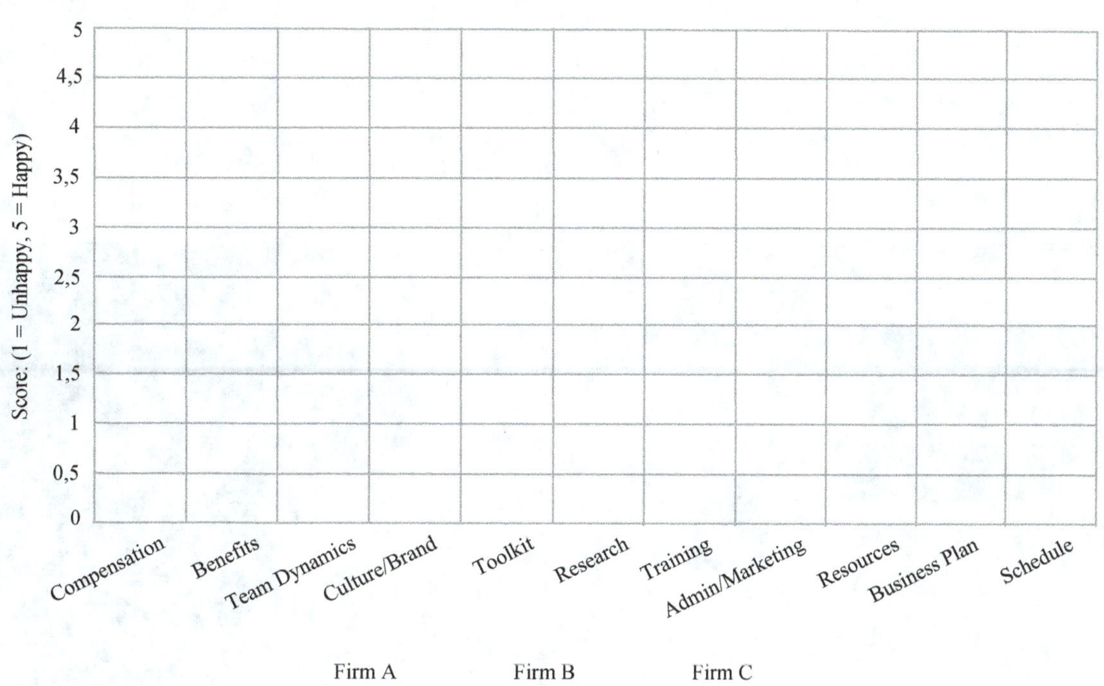

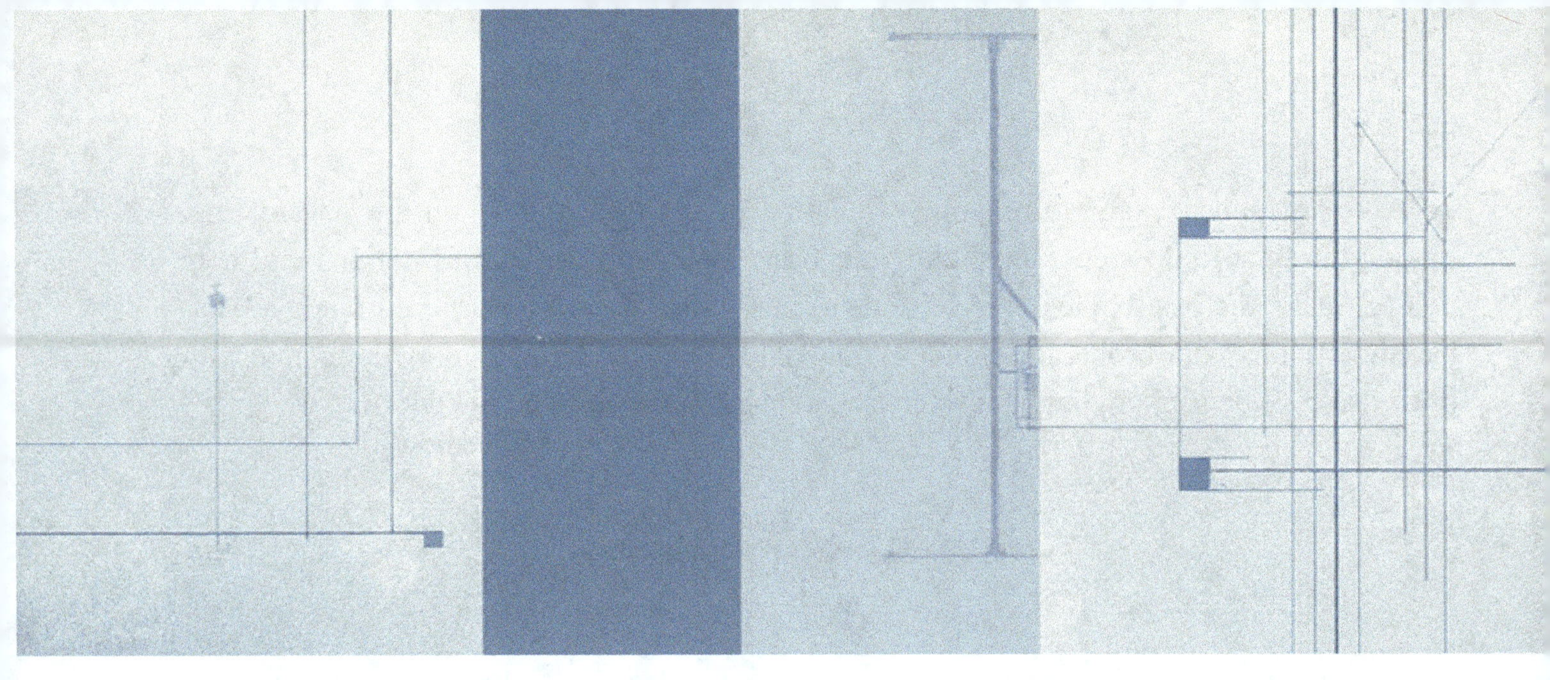

SECTION THREE:
ON SUCCEEDING

This section is where your career strategy turns into daily behavior. In Chapters 10 through 13, you move from choosing where and how you will play to executing with discipline, leverage, and confidence. You define your marketplace, your ideal client, and your personal brand, then anchor them in a clear purpose and a repeatable system. You learn that success doesn't come from flashy tools or scattered tactics, but from consistent front-door action, focused learning, and showing up the same way every week.

As you progress, you sharpen your execution with battle-tested systems for prospecting, follow-up, time management, technology, and sales mastery. You learn how to prioritize high-payback work, use data and tools to amplify, not replace, relationships, and build accountability habits that compound over time. The final chapter reinforces the quiet skills that separate good brokers from great ones: discipline, delegation, social confidence, and self-awareness. If you commit to the habits in these chapters, you stop chasing momentum and start creating it.

CHAPTER 10: SETTING YOUR SUCCESS STRATEGY

This chapter emphasizes that success in commercial real estate brokerage is built on consistent, direct action; the "front door" approach. While tools like email campaigns, AI, and social media can enhance your presence, they cannot replace disciplined outreach, follow-up, and market expertise.

It then explored five approaches to selecting a marketplace:

1. **Submarket/Area**: becoming a hyper-local expert through knowledge, farming, and community engagement.
2. **Radius**: focusing on a small geographic zone around recent firm activity to gain credibility and familiarity.
3. **Product Type**: choosing a category of real estate and developing deep expertise based on market supply and the relationship base.
4. **Vertical**: serving a specific industry (law firms, accounting, tech, etc.) to establish credibility quickly.
5. **Occupier or Asset Size**: specializing based on tenant or building size, becoming the go-to expert for that niche.

The chapter concludes by teaching how to build a personal brand around a chosen market and avatar—the ideal client—using consistent messaging ("four corners") and a clear broadcast path (speaking, writing, newsletters, podcasts, etc.).

CHOOSING YOUR MARKETPLACE

Marketplace selection can be based on submarket, radius, product type, vertical, or occupier/asset size. The right choice should align with your relationships, interests, and what your region has to offer.

Marketplace Selection Matrix

Complete the matrix below by ranking each approach from 1–5 based on your interest (1 = low, 5 = high). Then write a short reflection.

Approach	My Interest (1–5)	Why it appeals (or not) to me
Submarket/Area		
Radius		
Product Type		
Vertical		
Occupier/Asset Size		

Based on the rankings, which marketplace approach makes the most sense for your current stage, and what initial steps will you take to explore it?

CHOOSING YOUR MARKETPLACE

The chapter described the value of "farming": becoming a hyper-local expert who knows every asset, owner, tenant, and community leader in a defined area.

"Hot or Not?" Submarket Scoring Challenge

Step 1: Select Two Submarkets
- Submarket A:
- Submarket B:

Step 2: Score Each Submarket (1–5 per category)
1 = weak / low opportunity; 5 = strong / high opportunity

Criteria	Description	Submarket A	Submarket B
Asset Density	Are there many buildings to farm and learn deeply?		
Tenant Churn	Does the area have frequent moves/renewals (deal flow)?		
Landlord Diversity	Are there multiple landlords to build relationships with?		
Competitor Saturation	Are there many brokers already farming it? (Reverse-score: 1 = crowded, 5 = open field)		
Community Access	Ease of engaging Chamber of Commerce, business clubs, city leaders		
Personal Fit	Do you like being there? Would you show up consistently?		

Step 3: Add Total Scores

- Submarket A Total:
- Submarket B Total:

Step 4: Interpret Your Results

Which submarket appears stronger based on the score?

Did anything surprise you about your scoring?

What first three actions would you take if you chose the winning submarket?

You can create a radar chart comparison like the one below. This helps you immediately spot strengths, weaknesses, and opportunity gaps.

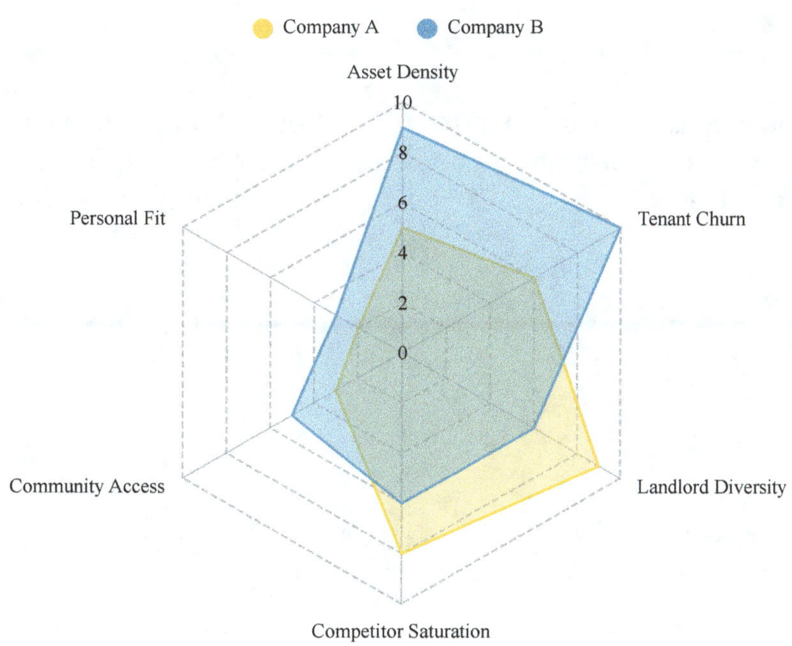

VERTICAL MARKET QUICK CREDIBILITY BUILDER

Verticals allow you to build credibility rapidly through focused learning using tools such as AI, trade associations, professors, and conversations with professionals.

"Rapid Research" Vertical One-Pager

Pick a vertical you might serve (examples: accounting, engineering, cybersecurity, law firms).

<table>
<tr><td>Key business challenges leaders in this vertical face.</td><td>How these challenges impact real estate decisions.</td></tr>
<tr><td>Questions you can ask a prospect in this vertical to demonstrate knowledge.</td><td>Initial data points you would want to collect (Sq ft per employee, space type, lease terms, etc.).</td></tr>
</table>

DEFINING YOUR AVATAR

Your avatar represents your ideal client. In the book, you learned about "Lucy," the CEO example, to show how understanding fears, goals, and context shapes your messaging.

Build Your Own Avatar

Fill in the template below.

<table>
<tr>
<td>Avatar Name:</td>
<td>Age:</td>
<td rowspan="3">Top 3 professional priorities:</td>
</tr>
<tr>
<td rowspan="2"></td>
<td>Role:</td>
</tr>
<tr>
<td>Industry:</td>
</tr>
<tr>
<td colspan="3">Top 3 frustrations or fears relating to real estate:</td>
</tr>
<tr>
<td colspan="3">How I (as a broker) can make them the hero: (Describe how your expertise helps this person win.)</td>
</tr>
</table>

DEFINING YOUR AVATAR

Your personal brand emerges from consistently communicating four core topics (your "four corners") across your broadcast channels (speaking, newsletters, LinkedIn, blog posts, etc.).

1 **Build Your Messaging Plan**

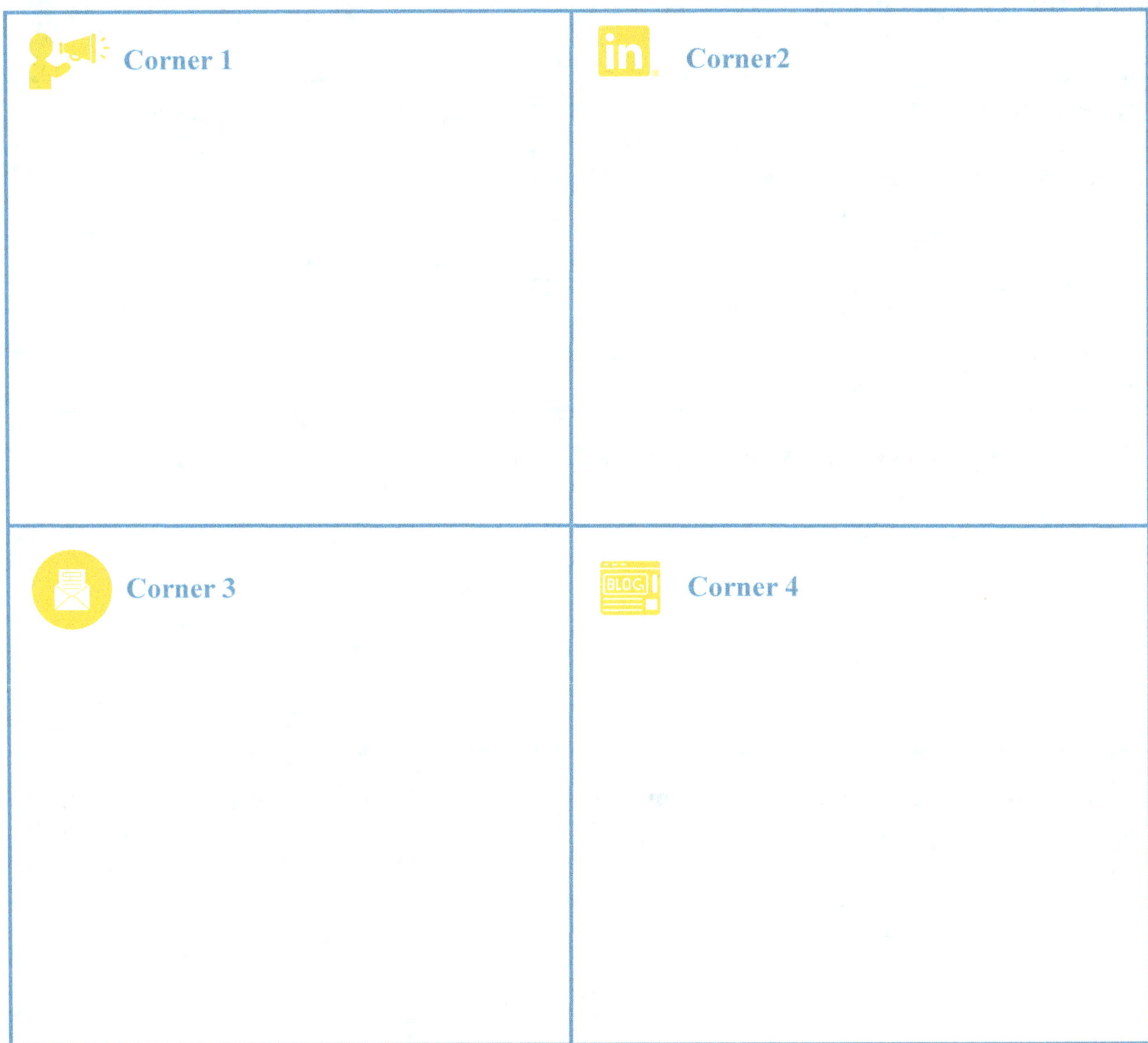

Choose two broadcast paths you will commit to for the next 60 days.
(Examples: weekly LinkedIn post, monthly luncheon speaking slot, short newsletter, local workshop, university guest talk)

Path 1:

Path 2:

Write a sample post or speech intro that includes one of your Four Corners.

CHAPTER 11: SETTING YOUR EXECUTION PLAN

PART A. THE WHY BEFORE THE WHAT

Successful commercial real estate execution starts with purpose, not tactics. Your goal is to help clients achieve business outcomes, not just complete transactions. Brokers who operate with purpose build stronger trust, better reputations, and more durable long-term businesses. Top producers rely on systems, not motivation or luck. Consistent activity, repeated over time, compounds into results. Your system should reflect your strengths, personality, and market, while being shaped by mentorship and real-world experience.

Strong execution also requires a deep understanding of clients and markets. Purpose-driven work means focusing on client success first. When you understand a client's business deeply and take satisfaction in their wins, discipline becomes easier to sustain over time. Rainmakers build simple systems early and refine them over time. What matters most is consistency, structure, and belief in long-term compounding effort.

Market mastery comes from field-level learning, not just database research. The more you understand buildings, ownership, tenants, and operational realities, the more valuable your insights become to clients. High performers also build broad relationship intelligence. "VIPs" are not just potential clients; they are market interpreters who help you understand economic, political, and business trends shaping demand.

ANCHORING YOUR "WHY"

Personal Purpose Statement Builder

1 **What excites you about helping clients succeed?**
(Example: Seeing a CFO win a promotion, helping a company solve a real operational problem.)

2 **What emotional reward do you want from this work beyond money?**

3 **Which values will guide how you show up as a broker?** *(Integrity, curiosity, persistence, service, something else?)*

4 **Which behaviors will reflect your purpose daily?**
(Ex: Making one extra call, asking deeper questions, preparing thoroughly.)

Draft Your Purpose Statement (3–5 sentences):
Write a clear statement summarizing why you do this work and who benefits.

DESIGNING YOUR FIRST SYSTEM

The chapter explained that rainmakers succeed because they follow a system, not a series of random tactics. Your system will evolve, but it must begin with structure, consistency, and a belief in long-term compounding effort.

System Blueprint Worksheet

Part A. What You Already Do Consistently
List 3 work behaviors you already practice with discipline.

Part B. What You Need to Add to Create a System

Choose 3 behaviors you need to practice daily or weekly (example: two hours of outreach, weekly follow-up block, weekly competitor review).

Part C. Build Your First Mini-System

Using the template below, design a simple 4-step system you can follow for the next 30 days:

Input: (What you will do daily or weekly)	**Process:** (How you will track it: CRM, spreadsheet, notebook)
Output: (Expected weekly metrics: calls made, meetings set)	**Review:** (When you'll review performance and adjust)

MARKET LEARNING "BUILDING CHECK SHEET" CHALLENGE

The chapter introduced a comprehensive building check sheet to help you learn your market deeply, including square footage, floor plate, tenants, ownership, debt, amenities, comps, and broker entry points.

Building Knowledge Field Study

Choose **one** building in your chosen submarket. Complete the following on a field visit or digital review:

Basic Profile
- Address:
- Size (RSF):
- Floors & typical floor plate:
- Ownership:

Operational Snapshot
- Parking ratio:
- Amenities:
- Leasing agency:

Tenants & Dynamics
- Major tenants:
- Which floors they occupy:
- Known move-outs or expansions:

Broker Insights

- What would be your best entry point to win a meeting?

- What immediate value could you add to a prospect in this building?

Reflection:

- What did you learn that you wouldn't have discovered from a database alone?

- What competitive advantage does this knowledge give you?

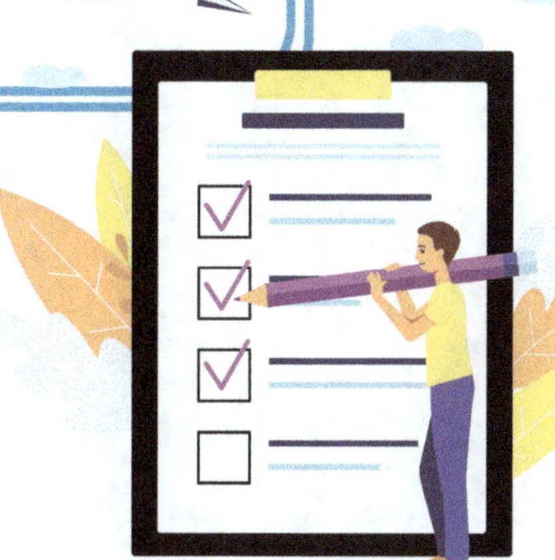

"Yesterday's home runs don't win today's games."
– Babe Ruth

THE VIP 50 NETWORKING MAP

You learned that "VIPs" include political leaders, editors, nonprofit heads, business leaders, landlord reps—anyone whose insight shapes your understanding of the market. Meeting them gives you intel and long-term relationship capital.

Create Your First VIP 50 List (Starter Set of 10)

List 10 VIPs in your market you would want to meet. (Hint: chamber leaders, economic development directors, transportation officials, business owners, landlord reps, editors.)
For each VIP, add:
- Why they matter
- How they could help your understanding of the submarket
- One personalized detail you can mention when you call
- Your plan for outreach (phone, event, referral)

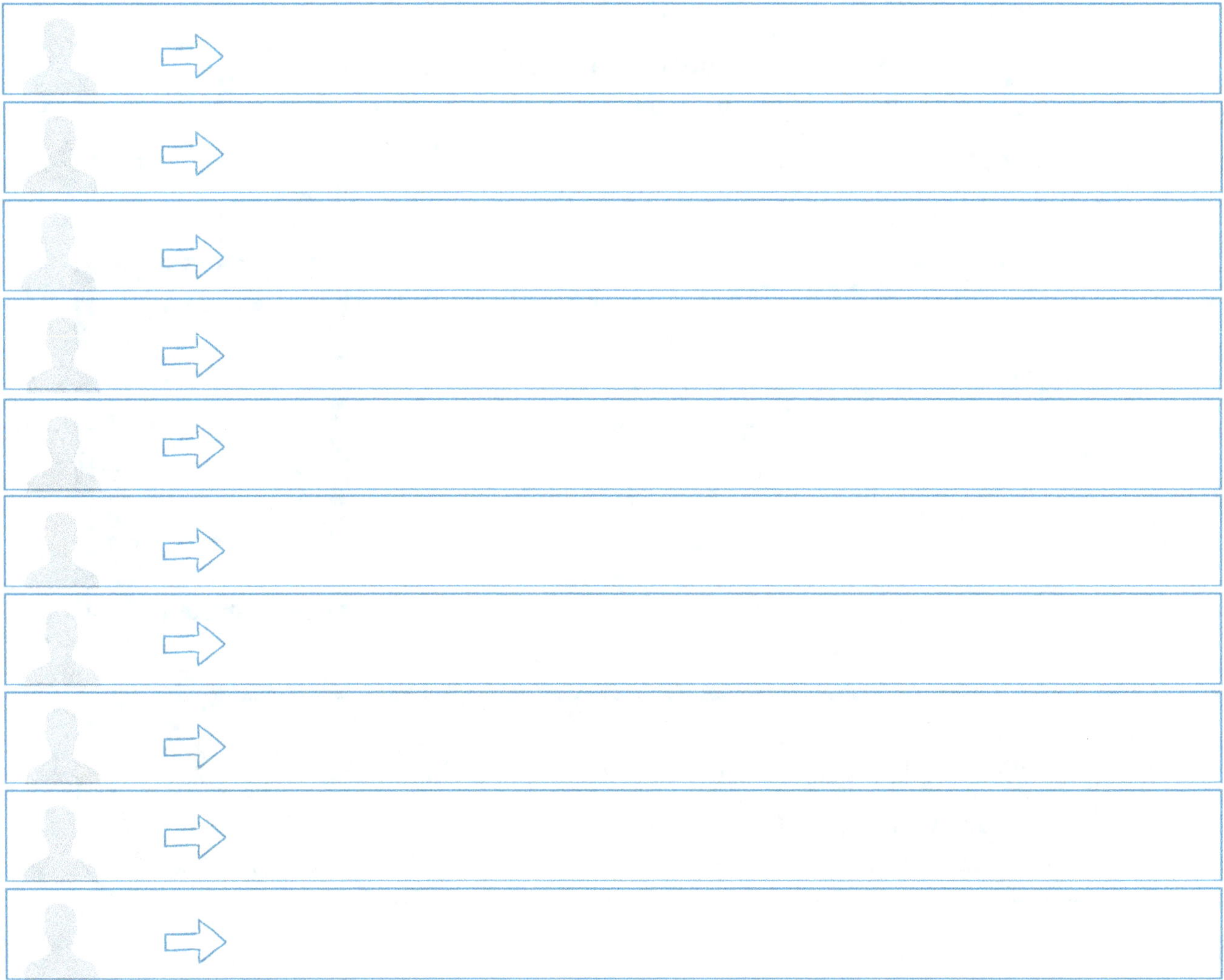

PART B. THE BATTLE PLAN FOR SUCCESS

Part B of this chapter gives you a practical, repeatable process for winning business in tenant representation. Inspired by John Cushman's "Find 'em, Mind 'em, Grind 'em," this section walks you through building your Business Development Battle Plan (BDBP), a system for identifying prospects, staying top of mind, and then winning when the opportunity arises.

You learn how to:
- Build a 400-prospect basket categorized into A, B, and C levels.
- Use a points-based accountability system to drive consistent effort.
- Create a structured call environment and daily routine.
- Follow a three-month roadmap to expand your basket, secure meetings, and close deals.
- "Push for the no" to handle rejection confidently and move efficiently.

These exercises help you build and customize your plan step by step.

BUSINESS DEVELOPMENT BATTLE PLAN FOR NEW BROKERS

Step 1: Build Your Prospect Basket

Your goal is to create a basket of 400 prospects, categorized into three levels based on their likelihood to need your services. Don't try to find all 400 at once; this is about starting small and acting fast.

Here's how to categorize and manage them:
Prospect Levels

A-Level Prospects (High Priority)

Definition: Companies with a high chance of needing your services within the next 30 days (e.g., expiring leases, known expansion needs).
Goal: Urgently secure a meeting with a decision-maker.
Action: Call, email, or visit to set up a meeting within 1-2 weeks. Be persistent but professional.
Mindset: Treat A-listers like they're "lucky" to be on your radar.

2   B-Level Prospects (Medium Priority)

Definition: Companies likely to need services within the next 12-14 months.
Goal: Build familiarity and credibility so they think of you when they're ready. Monitor for changes (e.g., expansion plans) that could bump them to A-level.
Action: Make initial contact (call or email) to introduce yourself. Follow up every 3-6 months to stay on their radar.
Mindset: Look for opportunities to "promote" them to A-level if new information suggests urgency.

3   C-Level Prospects (Low Priority)

Definition: Companies with long-term leases or no immediate need, but worth keeping an eye on.
Goal: Establish basic awareness so they know who you are "just in case."
Action: Send an introductory email or connect via LinkedIn. Check in semi-annually to maintain contact.
Mindset: These are your long-term bets. Stay professional, but don't invest too much time.

Tips for Building the Basket

- **Start Small:** Don't try to find all 400 prospects at once (no "boiling the ocean"). Begin with 10-20 companies in your submarket and expand weekly.
- **Sources:** Use LinkedIn, local business directories, or your brokerage's CRM to identify companies. Look for lease data or news about expansions.
- **Action Timeline:** Spend 1-2 weeks initially identifying 50 prospects (10 A-level, 20 B-level, 20 C-level). Add 10-20 prospects weekly until you reach 400.
- **Measurable Outcome:** By the end of month one, have 100 prospects categorized (20 A, 40 B, 40 C). By month three, aim for the full 400.

Step 2: Create a Points-Based Accountability System

Think of this system as "gutter guards" in bowling: it keeps you on track and ensures you use your time effectively. Be honest about your efforts; fudging the numbers only hurts your progress.

How it works:

Assign points to daily prospecting activities to measure your effort.

Example point system:
- **Make a cold call**: 2 points
- **Send a personalized email:** 1 point
- **Secure a meeting with an A-level prospect:** 10 points
- **Follow up with a B-level prospect:** 3 points
- **Connect with a C-level prospect (e.g., LinkedIn):** 1 point
- **Research a prospect (max 15 minutes):** 1 point

Daily Goal: Aim for 20 points per day (e.g., 5 calls, 5 emails, 5 research tasks).

Weekly Goal: Achieve 100 points per week and review your progress every Friday.

Tools

1. **Use your brokerage's CRM (e.g., Salesforce) or a simple spreadsheet to track points and activities.**
2. **Log calls, emails, and outcomes** (e.g., Left voicemail, scheduled meeting).
3. **Measurable Outcome:** By week 4, consistently hit 100 points per week and have at least 2 A-level meetings scheduled.

Step 3: Set Up Your Call Environment

Having a consistent setup helps you stay focused and professional during prospecting.

Workspace Checklist

Location: Choose a quiet spot (an office, a home desk, or a coffee shop with good Wi-Fi).
Gear: Phone, laptop, CRM access, notepad or tablet for notes, headset for clear calls.
Beverage: Grab coffee, water, or your drink of choice to stay energized.

Mindset Prep: Remind yourself:
1. "I have the best job in the world. Making calls and closing deals beats working in a salt mine!"
2. "My services are valuable, and these companies are lucky to work with me."

Call Schedule
1. Dedicate 2 hours daily (e.g., 9:00-11:00 a.m.) for calls and emails.
2. Block off time for research (30 minutes daily) and follow-ups (30 minutes daily).
3. Measurable Outcome: Make 10 calls and send 5 emails daily, logging all interactions in your CRM or spreadsheet.

Here's a three-month roadmap to build your basket, make progress, and start closing deals:

Month 1: Build and Start
- **Week 1-2:** Identify 50 prospects (10 A, 20 B, 20 C). Make initial calls/emails to 20 prospects.
- **Week 3-4:** Add 50 more prospects (total 100). Hit 100 points weekly. Two A-level meetings scheduled, 10 B-level follow-ups completed.
- **Outcome:** 100 prospects categorized, 20 points daily, 2-3 A-level meetings booked.

Month 2: Expand and Engage
- **Week 5-8:** Add 150 prospects (total 250). Make 10 calls/day, focusing on A-level prospects. Schedule site tours for A-level prospects who show interest.
- **Key Actions:**
  - **Site Tours:** Offer A-level prospects a tour of potential properties (aim for 1-2 tours by week 8).
  - **Follow-Ups:** Check in with B-level prospects every 3 months, and with C-level prospects annually.
- **Outcome:** 250 prospects, 4-5 A-level meetings, 1-2 site tours completed.

Month 3: Scale and Negotiate
- **Week 9-12:** Reach 400 prospects. Focus on converting A-level meetings into negotiations.
- **Key Actions:**
  - **Negotiation Stages:** For A-level prospects, move from meetings to proposals (Weeks 9-10) to signed deals (Weeks 11-12).
  - **Monitor B-Level:** Research B-level prospects for changes (e.g., news about expansions) to promote to A-level.
- **Outcome:** 400 prospects, 6-8 A-level meetings, 2-3 proposals sent, 1 deal closed.

Rejection is part of prospecting, but it's not personal. The "pushing for the no" strategy helps you stay confident and move on quickly.

- **What It Means:** Instead of fearing rejection, aim to get a clear "yes" or "no" from prospects. A "no" frees you to focus on better opportunities.
- **How to Do It:**
    - **Be direct:** "Is now a good time to discuss your upcoming lease needs, or should we reconnect later?"
    - **If they hesitate, push gently:** "I want to respect your time. If this isn't a priority now, can I check back in three months?"
    - **Accept "no" gracefully:** "Thanks for letting me know! I'll keep you in mind for future opportunities."

- **Mindset:** A "no" is a win. It clarifies who to prioritize and saves time. Celebrate moving on to better prospects.
- **Measurable Outcome:** By month two, aim for 5 "Nos" per week from A-level prospects to refine your list and focus on high-potential leads.

FINAL NOTES:

- **Stay Honest:** Track your points and calls accurately. Lying about your efforts only slows your progress, like cheating at the gym.
- **Stay Positive:** You're offering a valuable service, and every call brings you closer to a deal.
- **Act Fast:** Don't over-research. Start calling within the first week. Time is ticking!

By following this plan, you'll build a robust prospect basket, stay accountable, and turn rejections into opportunities. You've got this. Go make those calls and close some deals!

"We're not looking right now."

Response:

"Email me something, and I'll look at it later."

Response:

"We already have a broker."

Response:

"This isn't a good time."

Response:

"Maybe next quarter."

Response:

"We're staying put for the foreseeable future."

Response:

"Just send information—no call needed."

Response:

"We're cutting costs. No new projects."

Response:

CHAPTER 12: LEVERAGE TECHNOLOGY AND DATA: WORK SMARTER AND HARDER

Technology changes fast, but the purpose of your tools does not. As a carpenter relies on core tools, a tenant rep relies on digital tools that support relationships, manage deals, analyze data, and enable clear communication. Your tech stack should help you move faster, think smarter, and serve clients better. You must master the tools that matter most.
.

A strong CRM anchors your relationship strategy, while deal platforms keep transactions moving. Financial modeling, GIS, automation, collaboration tools, cloud storage, and eSignature platforms complete the modern toolkit. Business intelligence and social media help you understand prospects before you ever speak to them. The tools will change, but the core functions will not.

The 20/80 Principle reinforces that time is your most valuable, nonrenewable resource. To earn like a top producer, treat your time like top-producer money. Prioritize high-payback activities over low-value work. Over time, the goal is to trade value for money, not time for money. Sales is service. Great salespeople ask strong questions, understand motivation, tell clear stories, and build real relationships. Reading nonverbal cues strengthens your effectiveness.

Technology helps you work smarter. Time discipline keeps you focused on what matters. Sales skills turn effort into opportunity. Together, they drive consistent execution.

BUILD YOUR TENANT REP TECH STACK (YOUR CARPENTER'S TOOLBOX)

Create your personalized tech stack across the eight categories outlined in the chapter.

For each category below:

1. List what tool(s) you currently use (if any).
2. List one tool to research (ask mentors, check your firm).
3. Rate your current skill level (1–5).

Write the next action to improve your skill or adoption.

Category	Current Tool(s)	Skill Level (1–5)	Next Action	Deadline
CRM / Relationship Mgmt				
Deal Mgmt / Transaction Workflow				
Financial Analysis & Modeling				

Budgeting / Total Cost Tools				
GIS & Mapping				
Workflow Automation				
Collaboration & Scheduling				
GIS & Mapping				
Cloud Docs / eSignature				
Business Insight / Research Platforms				
Social / Professional Platforms (e.g., LinkedIn)				

Complete all rows and highlight the three most urgent tools you need to master in the next 90 days.

THE 2080 TIME VALUE CALCULATOR + HIGH/LOW PAYBACK AUDIT

To help young brokers understand the value of their time, I devised a simple exercise.

There are 2,080 working hours in a year: $52 \times 40 = 2{,}080$ (you can factor in vacation separately). To find your hourly rate, divide the compensation you'd like to make by the number of working hours in a year. For example, if your goal is to gross $1,000,000 per year (including paying your broker 50%), then $1{,}000{,}000 \div 2{,}080 = \$481$ per hour.

If you have the noble goal of earning $1 million a year, then let's double the $481 an hour and round up, so your time is worth $1,000 an hour in that scenario.

Your time is worth what your income goal demands. 2,080 hours/year.

A $1M income goal = ~$481/hour; rounded to **$1,000/hour mental model.**

Calculate your time value, then run a personal activity audit to classify your work into **High-Payback** and **Low-Payback** buckets.

Part A: Your 2080 Hourly Value

Write your desired annual gross income:

Divide by 2,080 hours:

Double it (mental model for opportunity cost):

Your hourly value: $ ____________ **/ hour**

Another lens I use is dividing activities into two groups: high-payback and low-payback.

Examples of high payback activities for me:
- Giving a speech in my community
- Taking a prospect to lunch or dinner
- Appearing on a business podcast that business leaders listen to
- Calling or otherwise connecting with large tenants who have leases expiring in the next two to five years
- Reviewing a lease on a deal I am working on
- Conducting a property tour
- Talking with a landlord and updating on market conditions

Examples of low payback activities for me:
- Completing expense reports
- Many meetings
- Completing a financial analysis (I have analysts for this purpose)
- Chasing unqualified leads
- Taking coffee meetings with people who want to "pick my brain" but cannot offer business opportunities

How you use your time will evolve as you advance in the business. Early in your career, you largely trade time for money, and your days may include many low-payback tasks, such as administrative work or support activities assigned by senior brokers.

As you gain experience, you should shift toward high-payback work and delegate lower-value tasks. Focusing on activities such as key client conversations and high-level business development enables you to trade value for money. This is the goal, and it supports both higher income and a stronger work/life balance.

List typical tasks from your last two weeks and categorize them using the chapter's examples. Then identify opportunities to delegate or eliminate low-payback items.

Using your hourly value, calculate the real cost of the following sample decisions.

Scenario	Time Spent	Hourly Value	Cost of Activity	Worth It? (Y/N) + Why
You spend an afternoon helping a client compare three different sublease options they found online.				
You attend a luncheon hosted by a property owner who wants to showcase their new building.				
You meet with a start-up founder who is unsure about future headcount and asks for guidance on space planning.				
You join a happy hour with several vendors from the CRE industry but no potential tenants.				
You prepare a financial analysis for a company evaluating whether to renew early or relocate.				

SALES MASTERY BUILDER: DISCOVERY, MOTIVATION, STORYTELLING, RELATIONSHIP SKILLS

Many people mistakenly view sales as demeaning or a last-resort career, but in reality, it's a noble, essential discipline rooted in persuasion, influence, and trust; skills that power leadership at every level, from CEOs to board chairs. When you treat sales as an act of service, it becomes a path to impact and leadership. Being able to read nonverbal cues is a ninja secret for getting people to like you and do what you would like them to do! Learn how to read others, and you will see your success go through the roof.

Great salespeople:

 **Ask great questions**

 **Understand motivation**

 **Tell concise stories**

 **Build likability and rapport**

 **Read nonverbals ("ninja secret")**

Write six questions you will use in future prospect conversations.

Choose one real prospect. Answer the following:

- **What pain are they trying to avoid?**

- **What aspiration are they trying to reach?**

- **What would make them take action in the next 90 days?**

Write a short, tight story describing a time you helped someone solve a relevant problem.

(45 seconds when spoken; 80–120 words.)

List five small acts of thoughtfulness you will use to deepen rapport with prospects:

Identify three nonverbal signals you will look for in your next meeting, based on Joe Navarro's framework:

"Never give up. Today is hard, tomorrow will be worse, but the day after tomorrow will be sunshine." – **Jack Ma**

CHAPTER 13: SUCCESS VIGNETTES

The success principles—accountability, discipline, prioritization, social confidence, and delegation— in this chapter represent the quieter skills behind top-tier performance. From weekly accountability calls and personal point systems to the Pareto Principle, cocktail-party strategy, and the "spinning plates" method of delegation, each vignette offers a proven technique you can implement immediately. Taken together, they reinforce a simple truth: consistent effort, thoughtful habits, and disciplined execution create the kind of "luck" that builds exceptional careers.

ACCOUNTABILITY 101: BUILD YOUR FRIDAY 5 SYSTEM

STEP 1

Choose Your Accountability Partner

Write the name of someone outside your industry who also has goals:
- **Partner name:**
- **Why they're a good fit:**

Define Your Goals

List 3–4 personal or business goals you want accountability for:
1.

2.

3.

4.

STEP 3

Write Your Accountability Questions

Create 3–4 questions your partner will ask you every Friday:
1.

2.

3.

4.

STEP 4

Schedule the Call
- **Day & time each week:**

- **Call length: 5-10 minutes**

Commit

Write a one-sentence promise to yourself:

THE POINTS SYSTEM: BUILD YOUR PERSONAL SCOREBOARD

Points System Gamified Challenge: Beat Your High Score

Rules of the Game

1. Choose 5 revenue-driving actions.
2. Assign each a point value.
3. Your goal each week: Beat last week's score.

Your Game Board

Action	Points	M	T	W	T	F	Total
1.							
2.							
3.							
4.							
5.							

Weekly Boss Battle

Last week's total: _______   This week's total: _______

Did you beat your high score? ☐ Yes ☐ No.

Why not? _______

THE PARETO PRINCIPLE: IDENTIFY YOUR GENIUS ZONE

80/20 Analysis Table

List Your Weekly Activities
Write 10–12 tasks you regularly perform:

1.

2.

3.

4.

5.

6.

7.

8.

9.

10.

11.

12.

Mark the Top 20% (Circle or Star)
Which 2–3 tasks create the majority of your wins, opportunities, or meetings?

Genius Zone Questions

What do you do exceptionally well?

What tasks produce the greatest return when you do more of them?

What do others say you're uniquely good at?

Write three commitments to increase your time spent on high-impact activities:

Write three tasks you will reduce, eliminate, or delegate:

Remember: 80% of your results will come from 20% of your actions.

COCKTAIL PARTY STRATEGY: CHOOSE-YOUR-OWN-ADVENTURE SCENARIO

You walk into a 90-person industry cocktail event. Music, clinking glasses, clusters of conversations. You have one hour.

Turn to the next question based on your choice.

1 **You spot someone you'd like to meet. What do you do?**
A. Approach immediately → go to #2
B. Wait until they're alone → go to #3
C. Circle the room first → go to #4

2 **You approach, and they're mid-story. Do you:**
A. Jump in with your own story → Outcome: You learn nothing. Restart.
 B. Smile, listen, and ask a curiosity question → go to #5

3 **You wait too long. They're gone.**
Lesson: Opportunities fade quickly.
Reset → go back to #1.

4 **You circle the room and accidentally shoulder-surf.**
Lesson: You're signaling disinterest.
Write 1 strategy to stay present:

Continue → go to #2

5 **You have a great 90-second conversation. What next?**
A. Ask for 30 minutes next week → go to #6
B. Leave on a high note and move on → go to #7

6 **They agree to meet.**
Write the follow-up you will send tomorrow:

7 **You end the conversation gracefully.**
List the 2–3 key details you learned to reference later:

Reflection: What did this scenario teach you about your event habits?

EVENT CHECKLIST

This checklist is useful when attending events where networking will be a key focus.

Pre-Event Prep

Who are 3 VIPs you hope to meet?
1.

2.

3.

What's your tailored USP or "elevator pitch" for this event?

During the Event

Check the skills you will practice:

- Use the 75/25 Rule (them first, you second)　☐
- Ask curiosity-driven questions　☐
- Avoid shoulder surfing　☐
- Make at least 1 helpful introduction　☐
- Limit each conversation to 90–120 seconds　☐
- Focus on building 3 high-quality connections　☐

After the Event

Write your follow-up plan:

- **Handwritten notes to send:**

- **Calls to make:**

- **Specific personal details to reference:**

DELEGATION BY SPINNING PLATES: THE DELEGATION SCORECARD

Effective delegation for complex, long-term projects requires giving clear, step-by-step direction and communicating a vivid picture of what success looks like.

1   **Clear direction:** Give precise, step-by-step instructions so your teammate knows exactly what to do, like following a detailed recipe.

2   **Define what winning looks like:** Define what winning looks like: Communicate a vivid vision of the finished product, using examples or visuals to show exactly what success should look like.

3   **Hold a 15-minute weekly spin session:** Meet face-to-face each week to review progress, maintain momentum, and show commitment to the project.

4   **Take detailed notes:** Document progress every week so nothing gets lost over time, using shared tools like Google Docs to track decisions and changes.

5   **Track reps on simple tasks:** For smaller assignments, review each version of the work to help your teammate improve until they can deliver high-quality results independently.

Rate Yourself (0–5) 0 = never / 5 = always

Delegation Skill	Score
I give clear instructions	
I define what "done" looks like	
I check progress regularly	

I stay out of the way while work is happening	
I coach instead of correcting	
I use shared documents to track tasks	
I delegate before I'm overwhelmed	

Total Score: _______ / 35

Interpret Your Score
- **0–14:** You're doing it yourself.
- **15–24:** You're delegating, but inconsistently.
- **25–35:** You're leveraging others like a pro.

Pick ONE Skill to Improve

Circle your weakest category.

Your 7-Day Improvement Plan:

Write one small action per day to improve that single delegation skill.

- Day 1:
- Day 2:
- Day 3:
- Day 4:
- Day 5:
- Day 6:
- Day 7:

Delegation Reflection: How did your workload and stress level change?

THE BROKER PERFORMANCE PRESSURE CURVE

To visualize how you respond to pressure throughout the commercial real estate deal cycle and identify targeted resilience strategies.

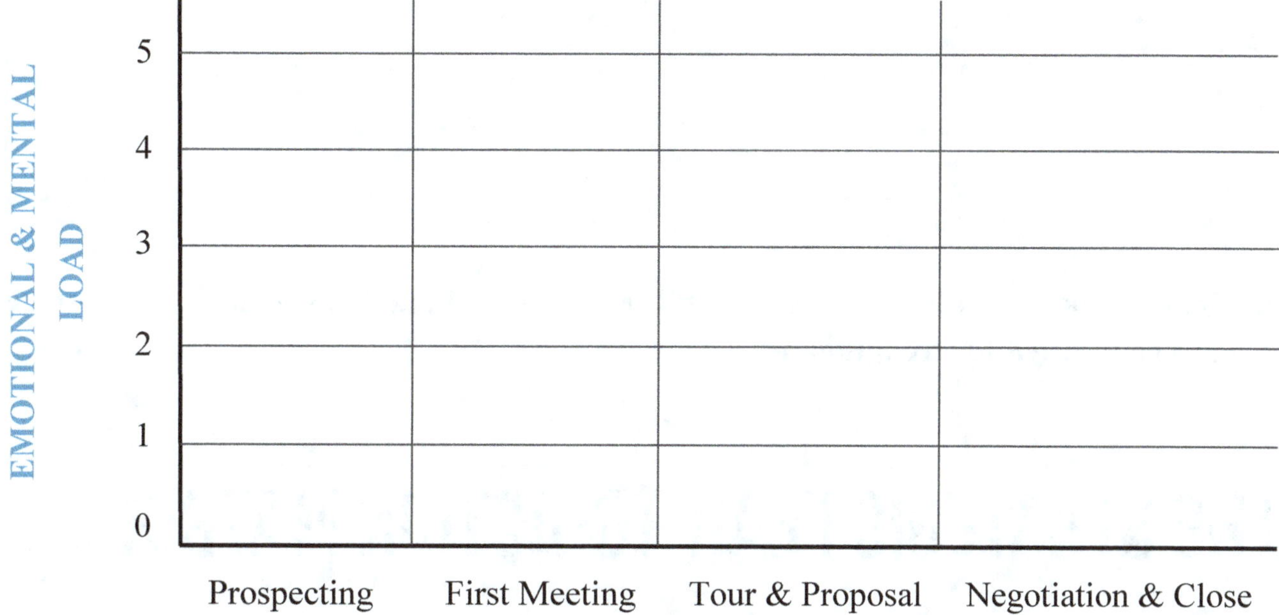

1. Plot a line showing how your emotional pressure rises and falls at each stage.

2. Add stress indicators:
- Long sales cycles
- Rejection or slow activity
- Difficult client conversations
- Performance expectations

3. List countermeasures for each high-pressure point, such as:

- Morning preparation routine
- Tactical listening review
- Scheduled micro-follow-ups
- Peer accountability
- Structured decompression time
- Add some of your own below...

6. Circle the point of highest pressure on the graph, and mark a star next to the stage you are committed to strengthening.

THE STRATEGIC FEAR-TO-ACTION MATRIX

We all have fears, but the key is not to let them get in the way of our own success. The first step in overcoming our fears is naming them and quantifying their impact on our ability to reach our goals. Then, putting an action protocol in place to overcome whatever is holding us back!

Fear Trigger	Operational Impact	Action Protocol
(Example: Prospecting reluctance)	(Example: Delayed outreach reduces pipeline velocity)	(Example: Daily 15-minute outreach block)
(Add your own)	(Add your own)	(Add your own)
(Add your own)	(Add your own)	(Add your own)

Examples of Items to Consider

Fear Triggers (Column 1):
- Prospecting reluctance
- Unpredictable income
- Negotiation pressure
- High-stakes client meetings
- Performance comparison with peers

Operational Impacts to Consider
- Pipeline slowdown
- Missed follow-up windows
- Overthinking or hesitation
- Reduced deal velocity

Action Protocols to Consider
- Standardized prospecting schedule
- 48-hour follow-up rule
- Client prep checklists
- Weekly financial review
- Tactical listening debrief notes

MARKETING & PERSONAL BRAND

Marketing in CRE is not advertising—it's your reputation before you enter the room. Your brand is defined by how others describe working with you, your consistency, your professionalism, and even your digital presence.

What do you think people currently say about you professionally?

What would you want them to say?

What needs to change to move from your current brand to your desired one?

Name three elements of your brand that you control and three that others perceive based on your behavior.

What digital footprints (LinkedIn, website, posts, etc.) currently represent you? Are they aligned with the image you want?

Draft your "brand descriptor sentence," a single sentence summarizing what you want to be known for in the CRE industry.

THE BROKER'S LONG-GAME BLUEPRINT

Purpose: To visually map the long-term arc required to build a successful CRE career and to identify the disciplined habits, short-term actions, and recurring checkpoints that sustain it.

5 Year Vision

Write a concise statement describing where you intend to be professionally. Consider:

Your role/title:

Your specialization or submarket:

Deal volume or income goals:

Your reputation and brand:

The types of clients you regularly serve:

The lifestyle or autonomy you want your business to support:

Break your 5-year vision into 4–6 measurable checkpoints. Examples include:

- Completing a certain number of tenant rep tours
- Joining or forming a top-producing team
- Developing a niche (e.g., life sciences, law firms, flex)
- Building a stable, predictable deal pipeline
- Completing one or more professional certifications
- Growing marketing reach (email list size, content cadence, event hosting)
- Add any other examples you can think of below:

Identify actionable priorities for the next 30 days that set your 1-year milestones in motion. Examples:

- Build or update personal marketing assets (bio, deck, website, headshots)
- Identify the top 50 target prospects and begin outreach
- Schedule intro meetings with market influencers or referral partners
- Block recurring calendar time for prospecting and research
- Organize CRM and build your next 90 days of pipeline focus
- Add any other examples you can think of below:

Translate your 30-day objectives into a tight, tactical one-week execution plan.
Examples:

- Complete 2–3 targeted prospecting blocks
- Attend at least one industry or networking event
- Prepare and post one market insight or useful content piece
- Review active deals and next steps with clear tasks assigned
- Reach out to 5 potential partners, COIs, or past clients
- Add any other examples you can think of below:

Weekly Non-Negotiables

List the behaviors and habits that keep you aligned with the long-term plan regardless of daily fluctuations in momentum. Examples:

- Minimum number of prospecting calls or emails
- Market research blocks (new listings, comps, tenant movements)
- Weekly broker coffees or networking touchpoints
- Deal or lease review time
- Social posting or email newsletter drafting
- CRM pipeline updating
- Add any other examples you can think of below:

Complete this sentence:

"My long-term success will be built on consistently executing __________________ every single week."

Every 90 days, revisit your plan to evaluate progress and adjust. Consider:
- What milestones have been hit?
- What actions drove the biggest results?
- What habits slipped and why?
- What new opportunities or challenges have emerged?
- What needs to be recalibrated for the next 90 days?
- Add any other examples you can think of below:

End each check-in with:

"My next 90-day focus is: ____."